MY NAME IS JOZEF BEDNARZ
Memoir of a WWII POW

Katherine Ritchie

Copyright © 2018 Katherine Ritchie
All rights reserved
First Edition

PAGE PUBLISHING, INC.
New York, NY

First originally published by Page Publishing, Inc. 2018

ISBN 978-1-64082-986-2 (Paperback)
ISBN 978-1-64082-987-9 (Digital)

Printed in the United States of America

To my father, a brave and courageous man, who loved the Lord and his family enough to survive Nazi imprisonment and see his dreams come true.

> The face of the Lord is against them that do evil, to cut off the remembrance of them from the earth. (Psalm 34:16)

> I sought the Lord, and he heard me, and delivered me from all my fears. (Psalm 34:4)

PROLOGUE

Jozef Bednarz was my father. My book tells the story of him growing up through an abusive childhood in Poland, imprisonment in concentration and labor camps during World War Two (WWII) in Germany, and finally, of his emigration to America and meeting my mom. My father described his life experiences and their effect on him, and I have passed on his words in this story as well as provided many pictures and documents he entrusted with me to share with others.

Our work together began with him telling me the details of his life events after he returned to Iowa from California in October of 2009, when he was seven months shy of his eighty-sixth birthday. From then on, he lived with my family for six weeks and we began to fulfill his dream of passing on the important aspects of his life in Poland and Germany as a boy and young man.

In the beginning of the project, Dad and I would sit together discussing his childhood and wartime experiences. The sharing sessions we had often lasted a few minutes to less than an hour as he grew tired and restless easily. At times the memories he recalled seemed to have been tortuous for him to verbalize, therefore I never pushed for the story to be told to me in any certain amount of time. I simply listened intently to my dad's words when he talked about his life and scrambled to jot down the words on whatever piece of paper I had available.

When I started to interview Dad, I tried using a tape recorder to do the interviewing, but he seemed agitated and uncomfortable. I grew concerned he might quit talking to me altogether, so I stopped taping his words and did not try to record our conversations again. I sensed that having a machine record his words was triggering the problem he had with paranoia.

Eventually, I hoped the scraps of paper used to hold the words of my dad's life story would become an epic account of his survival during a pivotal time in the history of the world. This has always been the goal of my persistence.

To my family, I provide a disclaimer that I have written a story about our dad's life according to what he told me and how I interpreted his words. Included on these pages are many of yours and other people's additions to the stories Dad repeated about his imprisonment during WWII and other life experiences. Due to the fact that our dad passed away before he could finish telling me the entire story of his life in Germany after the war, I used the pictures and documents he gave me to put this part of the story together, getting every aspect of the story 100 percent correct would have been an impossible task for me. I apologize to my family in advance for any inaccuracies I convey in the story.

During my time with Dad, he inspired me by his courage. He survived WWII as a Polish prisoner of war (POW), being held for over three years against his will in the Hamburg-Altona area of Germany. He was forced to work in concentration and labor camps doing hard jobs for the Nazis during this time.

While growing up, I knew very little about what my dad had been through in the early years of his life. The subject of his tortured previous years was never discussed within our family. I knew my dad was somehow involved in WWII. I learned more about the war in school that human atrocities of the worst kind had occurred. History classes taught me Hitler had murdered millions of Jews and defeating him had been a difficult task for the US and her allies. After I learned my own dad had been in Germany during the war, I always wondered how he had lived through those dangerous times, and now I find myself still pondering this part of his life more often.

As a young father in America, Dad worked extremely hard every day and helped my mom raise their children, but he never spoke about his old country or the war. Mother told us kids most of what we knew about his life. She told us he was a Polish emigrant and his life had been hard in the old country, although Dad had informed us all he felt we lived a life of luxury compared to the lives of his people who had faced many hardships in Poland for years and were continuing to struggle for survival. The other details of his past life seemed secretive or unimportant enough for him to share with us at the time.

When Dad moved in with me for six weeks after leaving California in 2009, he enjoyed watching WWII movies. I had assumed war stories would be traumatic for him to sit and watch. But no! He loved to reminisce about the battles of the great WWII conflict. He would explain some of the events to me and offer his opinions when we watched them. And then the personal stories would start. A scene in a movie would stimulate his memory, and he would ramble on about specific war memories. His movie watching activity proved to be invaluable in helping me to write his story.

After listening to Dad talk about his life, I wondered how his experiences had affected the way he raised me and my siblings. He could be a tough disciplinarian. We kids were made to behave without any slack. No matter that a few spankings came my way over the years, I still felt proud to be his daughter.

The credit for the idea of writing this book goes to my father. He asked me to write his story several years ago, and I believed it was worth the time and effort to complete the project, especially since my father's life has been a truly amazing journey for him. The suffering he endured during the early years of his life probably did energize him and help to promote the perseverance he needed to fight for survival during the toughest times of the war.

Dad would never admit he was a brave and courageous man, but he was to me. In spite of his bravery, the war left some brutal mental scars on him. Throughout his life, he never trusted the US government and always felt he was being watched. When he gave me one of his photo albums before his death, I found several pictures of him taken after the war hidden under pictures of his grandchildren. Not one was in plain sight! In spite of his lasting paranoia from the war, my father's story remains inspirational. Hope and faith in God were the keys to his survival.

Dad started to tell many people stories about his life as a senior citizen in his eighties. He talked more about his past life then than he ever had before. He would tell similar stories over and over again in the last years of his life to anyone who would listen to him. Because of his failing mind, he would forget what he had said and to whom he had told stories. Some people became irritated and bored by his repetitious reminiscing. Not me!

The storytelling Dad did later on in life proved to be therapeutic and provided a way for him to finally face his demons. I believe there may be other untold stories about the war and his life we may never know that are now buried with him in his grave! What we all will know are the details he told people about his life and of his courage, which are now repeated in my book.

Dad suffered from paranoia for much of his adult life. Today, doctors identify Dad's post-war emotional problems as post-traumatic stress disorder (PTSD). In my opinion, the wartime and childhood abuse my father suffered caused him great psychological trauma. Our family dealt with Dad's instability poorly over the years we spent with him. My parents divorced after twenty-three years of marriage due to his inability to follow prescribed medical treatment and his abusiveness to my mother and our family. I pray this book will help us all forgive him for the hardships he may have caused in our lives because of his own suffering and abuse.

Jozef Bednarz was a strong man and he is my hero. I feel my dad's story can be an inspiration to me, my siblings, my nieces and nephews, and future descendants yet to be born. His story may also provide encouragement to others who read about his life. There are aspects of the history of WWII some people may have not known and will learn in reading this book. I pray I have done my dad a great service if people become further educated about WWII through his story.

I have read many true stories and seen movies about the death and torture of Polish Jews during WWII. One of my motivations in writing this story was not to diminish their stories but to provide different information Dad wanted people to learn about the suffering and abuse of many other European people during the war. The hard times of his life, however, did begin well before Germany came to conquer Poland and continued for many years.

This is my dad's story as he told it to me. He did not have perfect grammar, so some of the explanations and descriptions I give reflect exactly how he talked! He had only an eighth-grade Polish education and spoke broken English.

There are contributions to my father's story in the book from my siblings, my mother, Leanne, my stepmother, Anne, Dad's friends, and anyone who may have heard one of his stories and had something to add. Any gaps in my dad's story are things he could no longer remember or did not tell anyone. Some details may have been left out or missing from his story because they were just too painful for him to think about and relive again.

My father left an impression on everyone he met. He greeted all people with a warm smile and a kind, firm handshake. When he met a lady, he reached for her hand and lifted it to his lips and planted a soft kiss on the skin while breaking into a charming smile meant just for her. He made all women feel special. Every greeting he gave someone reflected the strong Polish traditions he treasured.

Dad never compromised his fierce loyalty to Poland even after he became and remained an American citizen for over sixty years. The Polish traditions my father learned as a child were well ingrained into the person he became. His smile was bright and his laugh infectious. He had a strong Polish accent and a roaring temper and a stubborn nature. Jozef was a unique and kind person!

Jozef Bednarz was honored to be Polish and Catholic. He adored Pope John Paul II, who was also born in Poland. Dad's faith in Almighty God proved to help him survive the poor treatment in the concentration camps. He lived and died a proud Catholic and Polish emigrant.

My dad passed away before he could completely finish telling me his story, but we got through most of it. I miss you, Dad. I love you. I wish we could talk some more. This is your story.

INTRODUCTION

By Jozef Bednarz

November 2011

My name is Jozef Bednarz. I am eighty-eight years old. I am in good health except my memory is getting bad. I am chasing eighty-nine years. I was born in Poland. I immigrated to the United States from Poland by way of Germany after WWII in 1951. I have been very lucky in my life thanks to the Almighty God. I survived over three and a half years as a prisoner of Hitler's German government during WWII in Hamburg-Altona, Germany, after being taken forcefully by Nazi soldiers from my family's home at the tender age of seventeen. I was miraculously spared from death many times. After I was taken to the Nazi concentration camp, I could have been starved to death, tortured, or killed by bombs in a mere split second many times. I don't know why I lived. This is my story of survival as I told it to my daughter.

When I started to tell my life's story to Kathy, I was in good health. Now, I am eighty-eight years old. I sit with my daughter after a wonderful Thanksgiving and birthday dinner. I stare out into space wondering how my life has come to this. I know now how my life will end. I have cancer. The doctors tell me there is nothing they can do to stop the growth of the tumors in my body. They will keep me comfortable. I have pain in my bones. Sometimes, I cannot breath and I have to take treatments to give me more air. My brain is poisoned too. I don't know how long I will live.

I miss my mom. I can't wait to see her again, but I still pray to God to live. Miracles do happen, I told my doctor. He said, "Yes, they do." I have always hoped to live to age of ninety. Apparently, God has other ideas for me. What I want for now is to live as long as I can and enjoy my family. I will share most of the story of my life with Kathy as long as I am able.

In the end, the book will be about my life as told by my daughter. She will tell you how I have been blessed on this earth. I hope you enjoy my story.

CHAPTER ONE

The Early Years

On a cold day late in the fall, an angel of the Lord carried me to my mother's arms. Born in Brzesciany, Poland, a town located in the district of Sambor and the province of Iwow, I came into the world between WWI and WWII on November 27, 1923, to Barbara (Chlisczyck) Bednarz and Jan Bednarz. My father gave me the name Jozef.

My dad, Jan Bednarz

My mom, Barbara Bednarz.

Back then, Brzesciany, Poland, was a small agricultural town closely associated with the large industrial city of Sambor. Tall square gray buildings covered with rust-colored tile roofs lined the streets, emitting a musty smell that vividly scented the air, except where one passed by a bakery and the aroma of freshly baked bread aroused the senses. An abundance of stately pines and brushy shrubs provided a beautiful green color against the staunch monotony of the artificially manufactured landscape. This was my hometown!

As the years passed, my parents were blessed with six children. I was the oldest child and eventually had three sisters and two brothers. As the firstborn child of the family and a boy, I firmly believed life was far more difficult for me than for my other siblings. As the oldest and male, I was expected to help support our family by the age of ten. My responsibilities were endless before I was a teenager.

While I attempted to meet Dad's challenging expectations through all the work on the farm, I grew up quickly. In looking ahead at how my life played out, I matured faster than most children did at a similar age. My maturity probably benefitted me later on in life, especially during the war. As a teenager and wise beyond my years, war would eventually become a part of the future for me. I never thought much about this before, but when my father pushed me so hard doing farm work as a child and supporting the family, he may have helped me to survive the life-threatening experiences I had yet to be forced upon my life.

My father, Jan Bednarz, was a farmer and my mother, Barbara, took care of the house and the children. As one of their children, my parents expected me to obey them whatever the cost. Children were seen and not heard in this stubborn old country. No time for humor or just being a kid in their world, and obedience to them meant peace in our home.

Farming was a tough way to earn a living in Poland. Dad could not do all the farm work himself, so I helped him do chores every day. The older I got, the more I did and the less my dad did. As the years went by, Dad became a heavy drinker, and without mother doing her best to keep our family fed and clothed, I'm not sure we would have all survived.

My mother was a wonderful person. She tried her best to keep our family alive. She disciplined me and my siblings with a strict but fair hand. Dad, on the other hand, was not so nice, especially to me. I was bossed around the farm all day long and made to work so hard I felt totally exhausted at night. Eventually, when my younger siblings were old enough to do the farm chores, he would make me leave the farm and work in other places so he wouldn't have to feed me. His idea became one that I would make money to help the family out and take the pressure off him.

Life in the Bednarz home was difficult for us all because we were a poor peasant farm family. We survived by living off the goods we raised, grew, and sold from our farm. As I remember, the family farm was about ten kilometers or four and half miles from the city of Brzesciany. I knew about these miles to the town because I walked them many times with my dad. He forced me to go with him to town on a number of occasions to sell our produce and buy food for the family. I had to help him do this even though I was only nine or ten years old. Walking several miles to town was one of the first hard things I had to do as a child. Some days, I felt like my legs would fall off before we got home. I did not dare complain for fear he would punish me.

Back then, I know life for me in Poland was not like it was for children in America. At the age of nine or ten, I worked the same normal hours most adult men did. Dad started to teach me about man's work on the farm as soon as I could walk to the barn. I learned from experience I had to do what he told me to do or risk being beaten. When he did beat me with his belt, my backside would hurt for days. Quickly, I learned to never cross him.

At around six years of age, I dreamed of America. I knew I would go there to live someday. I had visions in my head of this great country being home for me. I started to think a lot about the special place so far away from Poland after I heard people talking about America in downtown Brzesciany. I never lost faith in my dream. I believed I would live in the USA one day even when I was suffering through hard times. I could have just been being silly hoping to go live there with the shape Poland and our family was in. I felt in my heart these aspirations motivated me to work hard for a better life. America would be my home in the future. I knew this and my knowledge filled me with happiness.

In our family of six children, there were three boys and three girls. After my birth in 1923, two girls were born after me. I loved having sisters. Unfortunately, without having brothers in the family, I had no one to help with chores on the farm and I never got a break. I did not complain and just did what I was told for my own good!

Aniela was my first sister to be born. Her name translates to Anita in English. She is about eighty-seven years old now and at a very good age to still be alive in Poland. Conditions in the twenty-first century continue to be poor in Poland and medical care is not good there. Aniela is lucky to remain strong and healthy at her age.

Aniela is a tiny person. Unbelievably, she exists under rough conditions and is living a tough life at her age. She resides in an apartment on the fourth floor of a building with no elevator in downtown Klodzko, Poland. The steps to her home are hard cement and the stairway is dark, cold, and gloomy. My sturdy sister walks down four flights of stairs to the street whenever she leaves her apartment and back up when she returns. Aniela's children and grandchildren look after her and help keep her stay safe.

My sisters: Aniela on the right and Bronia
on the left with their friends.

Katarczyna was born after Aniela. Her name translates as Katherine in English. Her nickname is Kasia in Polish and Kate in English. Katarczyna is a very common Catholic name in Poland and in my family. Both of my sisters have granddaughters with the same very beautiful name, as does Katherine who writes my memoirs in this book.

Although Kasia was the third-born child, she is the least healthy of my siblings today. She smoked cigarettes many days in her life and has had a couple of strokes as a result. Now she is about eighty-three and lives with her daughters Alicja and Urszula at alternating times. Kasia suffers every day from poor health.

Kasia's looks are similar to those of my mother. When angry, her eyes are piercing and almost black in color. These very dark brown eyes of hers and others in my family are unusual for people to have in Poland. Blue eyes are more common. Kasia, Bronia, Mom, and I all have brown eyes.

My sister Kasia and her daughter, Urszula.

I would like to tell you a story about the brown eyes of some of the Polish people. Most Polish people do have blue eyes and light colored hair. There is a reason for the change in eye and hair color of the Poles that dates way back in time. There is a legend I know of explaining the differences in the eye color of the natives of Poland. My people are generally known to have blonde hair and blue-eyes. The brown eyes and dark hair passed down through the ages after Genghis Khan came to my country from China. He raped our women, killed many men, and pillaged our land several centuries ago. His people were known to have the brown eyes. They crossed their soldiers with the women of my country. Now you can see how these changes have happened.

The birth of Stanislaw followed Kasia. He was my first brother. I remember the day he came into my life. Mom had carried Stanley for what seemed to me to be a very long time. One day, while Mom was still very pregnant, Dad sent me to the store to buy him cigarettes. I must have been six or seven years old (imagine buying cigarettes at that age). When I came back from the store, I heard a baby crying. Stanley had arrived.

Stanley was a good brother. When he grew up, he married Sophie from Russia. They were happy together. He worked in the coal mines for many years. Unfortunately, his job ruined his lungs and he got black lung disease. The last year of his life, he needed oxygen to help him breath. Eventually, he got colon cancer and had something wrong with one of his kidneys. The doctors never diagnosed the exact problem when Stanley died in September 2007. He was in his late seventies.

Stanley and I were very close. I called him quite a bit in the years before he died after he finally got a phone. When I visited Poland every couple years, I always stayed at his place with him and Sophie. When he died, I was extremely sad. I found out Stanley had died three days after I lost my son, Robbie, in 2007. Robbie was only the age of thirty-nine. This was a very hard week of my life. I couldn't believe I talked to my beloved son one night, and the next day he was gone. Three days later Stanley's children called from Poland to tell me he had died. I felt I had been tortured in my life when they died!

My brother, Stanislaw.

I really thought I would also die the week Robbie and Stanley died. My heart was broken in two. For me to have lost one of my sons and the only living brother I had left on earth was almost more than I could bear. I had to go to the hospital emergency room twice that week to get my blood pressure down. I tell you, their deaths hurt me more than the suffering I did during the war.

Bronislawa, or Bronia for short, was my third sister who was born after Stanley. Her name translates as Briana in English. Bronia lived a hard life. She smoked and drank a lot in her life and died from cancer at the age of fifty. The disease started in her esophagus and quickly took her life. I believe her death was her fault because of the way she lived.

As far as I know, Bronia had only one son. He and his wife came to visit me and Kathy in Poland in 1995 when we stayed at Stanley's house. This was a strange visit. His wife became very angry with Kathy because she could not speak Polish. She was screaming at Kathy in Polish and frightened her. Stanley got mad and kicked her out of his house, and Sophie freaked out and started taking some liquid in a spoon for her heart. What a wild night in Poland this was!

Other than this story about her son, I do not have much to tell about Bronia. I really did not know her well.

When Bronia died, my family buried her in the same cemetery plot with Dad in the Klodzko cemetery. This is the tradition seen in Poland where family members are buried together in the same cemetery plot in order to save money.

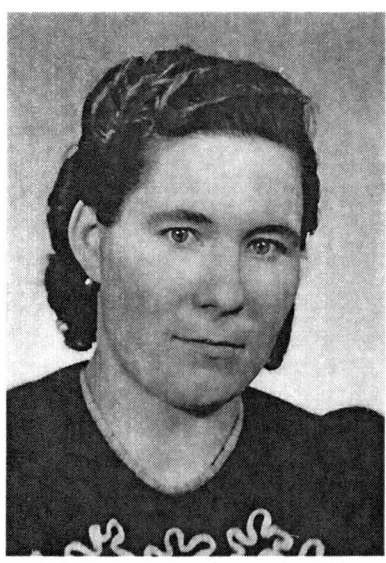

My sister, Bronia.

Miecxyslaw was another younger brother of mine and the youngest child born in the family. His name translates as Matthew in English. His shorter name Matteas or Metic used in Polish and can be translated to Matt in English. Matteas also lived a hard life in his adult years. He worked in the shipyards at Gdansk and fought as a professional boxer when he was a young man. The boxing profession left Matteas's face disfigured from scars caused by fractures and injuries he suffered during his career as a boxer. Being a professional boxer influenced Matteas to drink excessively and smoke constantly. His boxing carrier and marriage ended early, which I assumed happened because of his heavy drinking.

I don't think Matteas had any children. He never talked about kids and I never saw him with any children when I visited Poland. Matteas died in 1996 of lung and liver cancer when he was in his sixties. The last time I saw Matteas, he weighed less than one hundred pounds and stood about five feet tall. He was petite like Aniela, although the cancer had also shrunk him up.

Out of his generous nature and kindness to me, Matteas would ride the train from Warsaw to Klodzko all night to come and see me when I came to Poland to visit. He would bring gifts, which I knew he couldn't afford. My brother and sisters never trusted him. They told me he stole from them, but he was good to me. He died too young from a very hard life.

My brothers Matteas (left) and Stanislaw (right).

These are my Polish siblings whom I love and miss very much.

CHAPTER TWO

Challenges of Childhood

The first person I remember being most affectionate to me from the beginning of my life was my mom. We were close and I loved her more than I can say. She saved me from my dad's cruelty as much as a mother could. She was not mean to me like Dad could be. I compare her to Mother Mary, the Mother of God. In repayment for her sacrifices to our family, I vowed in my heart I would make her proud of me in everything I did all my life.

I hate to think of how Dad disrespected my mom on many occasions, especially while he drank cognac and vodka. He consumed these liquors whenever he could get them. Alcoholic beverages were readily available in Poland, and Dad always found a way to get them. As a result of his problem drinking, he made our lives much harder than they had to be. Mom and I accepted what happened with Dad and worked hard to help the family survive being poor and hungry.

When I got older, Dad looked at me as someone who should support the family for him. He never smiled at me or hugged me as an affectionate dad would act toward his son. He lacked concern for people in general, and I sensed his indifference. Sadly, I felt emptiness in my heart, never to be filled with joy at having a father who cared for me.

I ignored Dad's apathy toward me and focused on Mom and my siblings. I did what I could to help everyone live a better life by providing food to eat and fuel for heat in spite of how Dad acted toward me. I did what needed to be done for the good of the family.

Life for kids in Poland, especially for young boys like me, meant performing daily tasks normally done by grown-up men. There would be no time to play in the yard. I worked on the farm every day and almost every hour pitching hay and feeding animals. Before I was a teenager, I began to feel old and tired at the end of each long hard day's work.

Wood was a necessity for our family. We needed timber for fuel to burn in the kitchen stove for cooking and for burning in the fireplace to warm our home. Unfortunately, the laws in Poland were strict regarding cutting down trees in the forests. By law, a private citizen could not cut a tree down on public lands without permission from the authorities. In spite of the law, we had to go to the forest and use caution to obtain the wood we needed to survive. If we didn't cut the trees down and take the wood from the forest, we didn't have a way to keep us warm during cold winter nights or to cook our food. This dilemma we had to forget about so our family could live. We had to do what we had to do!

I remember some details about gathering timber even when I was a young boy. My dad and I sometimes walked together to the nearest forest to get wood. The best time to go there was when the sun disappeared from the horizon and the sky got dark. Even though the forests were owned mostly by millionaires who didn't really need the brown gold, they would not have liked us to be on their land stealing their wood. We had to be sneaky for our own safety.

At age six or seven, Dad started to take me to the forest to gather timber. We walked a couple of kilometers—a long way for me to walk to get the wood, but my dad made me. I had no choice. Again, I knew he would beat me if I complained. What was the use in that? Anyway, my sacrifice was for the good of the whole family. We went to these great lengths since we didn't have any good firewood on our own farm. This is why we went to the forest and took what we needed for fuel.

Dad taught me lessons about being careful in the forest. Dangers lurked everywhere. As we walked, Dad would tell me what to watch out for. There might be animal traps or mountain lions or people to beware of. Remembering what he told me would be necessary in the future for me to protect myself when I went there on my own.

Dad would instruct me, "You have to walk quietly, Jozef. Try to walk on the leaves. The dry branches crackle under your shoes and make noise. Someone might hear us or you might trip and fall." He lectured me on numerous occasions.

"Yes, Father," I whispered, careful not to raise my voice and alert any guards in the area.

There were acres of woods in the forest. The trees were large and threatening. Their tall, ghostly shadows leaned toward us shaking, with their spindly fingers in our faces. I dared not stray far from my father lest the wiry spirits of the dark might suck me into oblivion. I stayed close to Dad, surely not wanting to get lost. At my age, I was still afraid of some things, particularly of the darkness deep into the trees. Additionally, I heard lots of weird noises different than those on our farm. Having a familiar man next to me during times such as these when I felt my bravery being challenged made me feel much more secure.

Dad and I hid easily among the immense trees and thick underbrush as we took the wood and headed home. We piled crusty branches high on our necks and snuck through the woods to the dusty country road leading us to safety. With Dad's foolproof plan in action, we never got caught taking the sturdy cordwood from the forest when we were together.

When I grew old enough to be trusted out on my own, Dad would often send me outdoors searching for food for the family. I went hunting for supper beyond the boundaries of the farm. There were forests to hunt in and rivers to fish in. As long as I was away trying to bring home a meal to put on the table, Dad would not bother me, and I felt much happier about life.

The best ways to get food for our family were to fish and hunt. I hunted for rabbits and squirrels. I went fishing for whatever I could catch. My sisters, Kasia and Aniela, would help me out to do what they could to feed the family when they were old enough. Eventually, Stanley helped me hunt and fish when he got older. We all pitched in to provide what my father could not, did not, or would not to help us survive. What a heavy burden for young kids!

I remember we had a few fruit trees on our farm. The luscious apples and pears were good eating. Aniela, Kasia, and I picked the produce off the branches and ate some if we were real hungry. We had to save what we could to be sold in town to get money for supplies needed on the farm. And we gave what remained to Mom for baking and making salads. These trees were good to us and beneficial to our lives in so many ways.

Do you know how we got those fruit trees? Before we had a way to feed ourselves off the land other than the crops we grew, I went into the edge of the forest to eat the fruit off the trees. I think I was eight or nine years old when I first started to do this. After eating the juicy reward of my grueling stroll down the hot rocky road, I would dig up the higher yielding plants found in the forest and bring them home for planting. After a few years, our family had fruit trees to help feed us and ease our hunger.

The fruit trees on our farm were mostly apple. They were real juicy and a great treat for us kids in the summer. We picked as many apples as we could reach and gave them to Mom on days no one went to town. I loved the apple pies my mom would make when she had enough flour and sugar. The smell of her desserts baking in the kitchen was like heaven to us all.

At about age ten, I started going to the forest to get wood by myself. I had to be sneaky as my dad had taught me and be careful not to get caught when I took the baby fruit trees and the firewood. I could never forget the rich people in Poland who owned the forests and had the security guards watching over their precious commodity. When in the forest alone, I pretended like I did with my dad being quiet with the wood and cautious with every step I took. The wood felt heavy on my small shoulders. Painfully yet stealthily as possible, I carried the treasure out of the forest on my neck. Incidentally, little did I know at the time, carrying this wood on my back would help make me strong for the hard labor I would do during the war.

The summer was a pleasant time to get the wood from the forest. Winter was another story. I had to walk many rough miles through the deep snow and carry the firewood home feeling heavily burdened. Fortunately, I always got home safely without freezing to death.

Aniela and Kasia didn't go to the forest with me until when they were older. When they did finally go to the forest, they carried the smaller pieces of wood home. These were very hard times for our family as peasants in a country where we simply did what poor people had to do in order to stay alive. I felt gratitude to have the help of my sisters to accomplish this goal.

When we got home with the wood from the forest, Dad and I had to hide the logs in the barn under the straw. We could not take the chance anyone would see it. Getting caught with the stolen timber could cause serious punishment to our family by the police for breaking the law, thus making a bad situation worse.

I wasn't always so lucky taking the wood safely from the forest. Once, I did get caught at about age fourteen. In the forest by myself, I was cutting a branch off a fallen tree when I encountered a problem. The Russians had been using this logging site during the day and had left before I arrived. Some wood lay recklessly strewn around, so I decided to clean up the kindling lying loose on the ground. This was easy work for me this time, and I appreciated the break. Unfortunately, I was interrupted.

While cutting a branch off of a fallen tree, I heard someone yell at me.

"Who is out there? Stop," a voice screamed in the darkness.

When I heard the voice in the dark yelling at me, I knew I must have been seen. I started to run as fast as my little legs could carry me, but I never made it out of the forest.

Before I could exit the woods and reach the safety of the dirt road to our farm, the police arrived to block my progress. Someone had seen me and reported my illegal presence in the forest to the authorities. Whoever saw me must have thought I cut the tree down myself illegally. Cutting down a tree without the permission of the landowners was a crime as was taking any wood from the forest!

After being arrested in the forest that night, the police took me home to my parents. Later on, charges were filed against me in

Brzesciany at the police station. The authorities informed my dad I would have to go to court to face the charges for cutting down the tree.

Since I was too young to go to court by alone, my mom had to go to court with me. What a frightening experience this was for me at my age.

The judge looked very mean, and I feared I might be harmed by him. Mother saw my distress and comforted me before the officials of the procedure called my name to face the black-robed man in the big brown chair. Mom assured me I would survive the horrible ordeal if I kept quiet and stayed respectful to everyone.

"You took wood from the forest?" the red-faced judge growled toward my face.

"Yes, sir," I said, my body trembling from head to toe.

"Don't do it again. I will put you in jail next time." He stared at me with piercing unforgiving black eyes.

"I won't, sir," I whispered in a barely audible voice, knowing I would be more careful in the woods from then on.

Fortunately for my family, the judge dismissed the charges against me for cutting down the tree in the forest. This was a good thing. We didn't have any money to pay a fine. Happy to be pardoned by the judge, I listened intently to his warning. He did tell me if I got caught cutting down trees in the forest or stealing wood again, I would have to pay a fine or go to jail. I knew he had no reason to be kidding.

After the bad experience in court, I laid low for a while. After being arrested for my mistakes in the forest, I became more careful than ever.

Dad was very unhappy I got caught taking the wood. He lectured me sternly.

"Jozef, I taught you better how not to get caught in the forest," he preached.

I knew I had to shake off this setback and continue to support my family because most weeks my parents didn't have much money to buy groceries. Our family's hunger motivated us all to find food for each other to eat. We ate the fruit from the trees on the home farm and roasted wild rabbits we trapped. Catching those fluffy animals had to be done in a special way. I will tell you how we did it.

My sisters and I would go into the forest on nice days and catch rabbits to take home and eat. Their quickness made our task a tricky process. In order to entangle them, we would tie a thin wire across the lowest part of the tree trunks. When the rabbits would run into the sharp line, they would cut their throats. Then we would have them and food for supper. Honest—I tell you, this is a true story!

We would take home seven or eight dead rabbits on some of the hunting adventures we completed successfully. Our family ate the meat off their bones and saved the skins to sell. The protective covers of those fat bunnies brought good money in town. The cash enabled our survival especially when winter approached. Our family always found a way to do what we had to do to stay alive.

We made money for our family in many ways. Selling our farm goods in town helped us financially the most. Dad and I would walk with our produce from the farm into the nearby village. We sold eggs and milk to the townspeople for a generous price. We had certain customers who bought these products, and the monies we made in town were a blessing to our family. People in town came to know us and trusted the goods we had to offer.

Catching fish was another fun way for me to bring home a meal for the family to eat. I loved to go fishing even though the river was a long way from our farm. I had to walk about three or four miles to get to the river. I didn't even care about the long hike. In the end, I was doing everyone a favor and getting a break from the farm when all the chores were done.

On my way to the river, I listened to the birds singing and smelled the sweet fresh air as I skipped along the path. I slung my fishing pole over my shoulder and away I went, whistling or humming all the way to the Dniester River. No one was there to bother me during the times I went by myself. Sometimes, life was good!

When I got to the gleaming blue waterway, I would put the bait on the hook and throw my line into the river. I used night crawlers to tempt the appetites of the fast swimmers below the water. This worked pretty well for me. The fish and the ducks would usually take the bait and swallow the hook.

When I caught a fish, I felt happy, like I had done a good thing for our family. I would bring a string full of perch and carp home for supper on many days I fished. (I was a pretty good fisherman!) I cleaned the fish, and my mom cooked them up. Delicious!

When I went fishing, sometimes I caught fish and other times I snapped up the ducks. I had good string on my pole, so if I caught a duck, I could pull him in. Some of the ducks were really fat and strong. When the ducks swallowed the bait, they fought hard to escape. I would catch the wild ducks just like I caught the fish and reel them right into shore. I took whatever I would catch home for supper. I loved to see mom happy with me and smiling when she saw a duck tied on the stringer.

Incidentally, a good friend of mine from a high class Jewish family got shot and killed at that river. The Nazi soldiers murdered him for no reason. He was like a boy scout and better educated than me, but we still got acquainted. We stayed friends until we were separated during the war. I never saw him again once the war started. I felt really bad when I heard he died. He was an innocent Jewish boy. I guess they murdered him because of his religion.

So my life as a young boy in Poland was hard, but others did not even survive their youth.

CHAPTER THREE

Born Catholic

I was born and baptized a Roman Catholic. My parents were strict about religion and our family practiced Catholicism faithfully. All of us kids were made to kneel on the cold cement floor at our bedsides and pray the Our Father every night and sometimes in the morning. We went to Mass on Sundays and holydays of obligation. No excuses for an absence were allowed by them.

Active participation in the sacrament of Confession on a weekly basis became another part of the religious faith I practiced when I was about seven years old, just before I received First Holy Communion. In order to fulfill our commitment and be pure in the eyes of God, I along with the family went to confess the sins we had committed against Him. Reconciliation, or the Sacrament of Confession, involved talking to a priest in the Confessional room at church on a Saturday afternoon before any of us were allowed to go to church Sunday morning and receive the Sacrament of the Eucharist after we had received our First Communion. My parents demanded our family take part in the priestly pardon of any wrongdoings we had committed during the past week.

Confession comprised of a mostly bad experience for me. I could always feel the pounding of my heart through the chest wall of my body as I walked into the beautiful statue-filled church. The saintly stone figures glared at me with deep protruding eyes as I dared to enter the church in a state of sinfulness. Their gazes followed me, the sinner, deep into my soul in a creepy sort of way. I was taught my salvation could be attained with the proper begging of forgiveness from the priest, but first I had to get past these eerie statues.

In spite of any physical discomfort in the church, my parents made me go through the Confession regiment before I attended Mass services on Sunday. Dreading the feeling of shame I had each time I walked into the threatening environment to whisper to the priest the wrong deeds I had done, I knelt down on the hard wood kneeler, confessed my sins, begged for forgiveness, and accepted my penance. Whew, good for another week but not really that simple.

The confessional could bluntly be described as a tiny dark room, which one entered by slipping between two long black curtains. Inside the dimly lit space was a hard slab of wood intended for the accused to punish their knees while kneeling in a bent position pleading their regret for sins committed against God. Once positioned in a somewhat painful manner, the sinner faced a wall containing a sliding screen window separating him or her from the priest who would order an examination of the confessor's conscience. Shame and seeking pardon were the reasons for lowering one's self-esteem and entering the turf of this holy person authorized to represent the Lord Jesus and provide forgiveness and penance.

On most Saturdays, I walked into the close quarters of the private confessing space and knelt down on the hard pine kneeler. The priest would slide the small wooden trap door open with a deafening slam and allow cold air to fill the darkness surrounding me. The musty smell of his old black garments would sting my nostrils, however, the scent of the burning candles somewhere in the air behind him did provide me with some sense of security. Then it was time to begin and I would start to sweat.

In the shadows behind the screen, the priest would lift his hand and make the sign of the cross parallel to my face as we started the painful ritual.

"Bless me, Father, for I have sinned," I begged in a barely audible tone of voice. "My last Confession was one week ago." I murmured in disgust of myself.

With his ear close to the screen, the priest listened to me tell him the bad things I had done over the past seven days. When I finished my Confession, I braced for his mean words about my actions.

"Young man, you should know it is wrong to steal. Only bad kids take what does not belong to them. God sees what you do and he is very angry." His gritty voice pierced the silence of the chilly, damp closet-sized space of the confessional as he spat the moist stern words through the screen at me. I cringed awaiting the consequences of my admission of guilt.

Wiping away the dampness from my face, I listened to the Holy man's attempt at forgiveness of the sins I had committed.

After several minutes of fatherly lecturing, the man in black with a stiff white collar finally told me to say ten Hail Marys and ten Our Fathers for penance. The idea of the fervent praying was to save my imperfect soul from the final damnation of hell after I died. Additionally, he had attempted to keep good control of my behavior by making me fearful of God.

During Confession, I told the priest I had taken wood from the forest. Stealing was a sin and also a dilemma for me. I knew taking timber from other people was wrong, but I had to steal the wood for the welfare of our family. I had no choice. I knew God would forgive me. The priest did not seem to want to let my innocent indiscretion go. He and every other priest had yelled at me for stealing. They all believed I was bad. I wondered how they would feel if they were poor like my family and I. Somehow, I knew in my heart God understood why I did what I did.

Even though I hated going to Confession, being a good Catholic was important to me. My parents taught me about the Almighty God and prayers to honor Jesus and His mother. I felt grateful to them for the spiritual values they bestowed in me. Looking back on the life I have lived, I can conclude God did protect me all my life as a result of being devoted to Him. I have never stopped praying for courage and strength to do His will.

During my life, I never missed church on Sunday unless I was too sick to go except during the war. Not often, oh, not too often was I absent from church. I owed God my life and being a faithful

Catholic was the least I could do to repay my Savior. My faith was tested long before the war. As a young child, I was given reasons to doubt the existence of a loving God in the world. Catholic school would present the first spiritual challenge to me. Polish Catholic leaders had strict religious educational rules in the early 1900s. As a result of the rules, parents were strongly encouraged to have their children educated in parochial schools. Therefore, my parents sent me to a Catholic school when I was about eight years old.

In order to reach the Catholic school, I had to walk several kilometers by myself. Although I had been to town with Dad many times and I knew the way, I was still uneasy about the daily weekday journey to an unfamiliar place I came to quickly dislike. Although I temporarily escaped the cruelty of my father's treatment, I gained a new evil to contend with. As I will explain, attending religious classes in town became just another hard thing I had to learn to do and accept in life.

When I started to go to Catholic classes, I thought I would be going to a normal school. After I found out what that school was like, I became afraid to go back there day after day. The priests and nuns were not nice to me. Eventually, I did find out why they were so mean.

After a few days at the school, I realized there was a tradition happening in this grand-size building of Catholic education. There was an expectation for the students to bring gifts for the nuns and priests who were their teachers. Obvious to them, we all needed to pay a price for their teaching us. However, my family was poor and I could not bring gifts for the teachers like most of the kids were able to do.

The Catholic teachers felt they all deserved the special surprises provided by the students. Those classmates of mine who brought gifts were treated better than the ones who did not. Since I couldn't bring anything extra for my educators, I had to be punished and failed to understand the logic of the holy Catholic school I attended.

One day when I went to class, the students brought in warm cinnamon rolls and other sweet treats for the nun seated at the simple wooden desk under the chalkboard. And, as usual, I did not bring her a gift and I knew there would be trouble as soon as I came through the classroom door. The old woman dressed in black had her eyes on me. I felt trapped.

The stern nun passed through the aisles of the classroom heading in my direction with only her frowning white face exposed through the tightly fitting habit enclosing her hair and ears. When she arrived at her destination, suddenly she halted. I shivered, knowing I was in trouble once again.

"So you bring me nothing?" she growled at me in her strong Polish voice.

I looked down into my lap and felt bad. I had nothing to offer her.

She could see I came empty handed.

Smack! She slapped me across the face for not bringing her a reward for her efforts.

"Will you never learn?" she barked at me and moved on.

The red mark left on my tender face burned like fire. The pain in my heart stung worse. Being a little boy at such a young age, I did not understand the mean psychology of some people in the world. I did nothing wrong to be hit by this nun! There was not a thing I could do about my situation. I was helpless against her wickedness.

The nuns were poor and I did not blame them for wanting gifts from their students. I still believed they should not have been mean to me since I did not bring them special things. I was a disadvantaged student, however, my behavior in the classroom proved to be good. I believed what happened to me at this school was wrong. In my mind, nuns and priests were supposed to be good people of God. After these incidents, I mistrusted some of the clergy in the churches I attended until later on in my life when I met nice priests and nuns who were not like the teachers I knew as a child in Poland. They were unusual people. Another example with a priest I knew will show more of what I mean!

Once a week, instead of the nuns teaching us, the priest from the Catholic Church in Brzesciany came to our class to speak about religion. I didn't like him because he also punished me. In one incident, I didn't bring him a gift and he embarrassed me in front of the students.

"Jozef, go!" he yelled to me as he pointed to the table in the back of the classroom. He took my arm and roughly dragged me behind a large wooden desk in our classroom. There was no reason for him to punish me. I had obeyed whatever he told me to do. His treatment of me was simply unfair.

On one particular day, when the priest was the teacher at the school, I had to stay for one hour behind the chalkboard. The next week, he came and the same thing happened again. This time, an hour went by and he never came back to let me go free.

I told myself, *Enough of this disgraceful treatment.* I had an idea to stop all the bullying.

Well, the chalkboard in our classroom was huge. This priest couldn't see me behind there. I put my plan into action and escaped from his class. I slipped out of the classroom before he knew I was gone. He didn't know I had left, or I'm sure he would have chased me back in. At this point in time, I knew I certainly didn't ever want to go back to be beaten by him.

I went home after I left the priest's class and told my parents all about what had happened to me at the Catholic school. Mom and Dad figured out why they punished me at the school even though I was a really good student. My parents knew this and trusted my story.

Mom and Dad never made me go back to that Catholic school again after I told them all the bad things the nun and priest teachers did to me. I was happy not to have to return to that religious school. The priests and nuns had made me mad to them, but not to the Catholic religion or to God.

CHAPTER FOUR

Adopted Out

During the times I did not attend normal school, I had to help my dad make hay to feed the horses and the two cows we owned. I worked in the fields with him after the animals were fed. The farm chores never seemed to end for me. When I entered school every fall, Dad would not be happy because he was forced to do more of the farmwork. Eventually, my going to school would be meaningless to him, and I would not be allowed to continue my education after age fourteen.

As I grew older, using the farm tools became second nature to me. Dad had a razor-sharp scythe he taught me to use to cut the hay. While swiping the grass with the dangerous tool, I would be chased by him to the front of the field, causing us both to go faster and make the work harder yet more productive. Some days I thought death from exhaustion might be my welcome fate right there in our unwelcoming tortuously hot field.

On many hot summer days, after several hours of swinging the scythe, the thin arms of my body felt like heavy weights pulling the weary shoulders of my frame out of their sockets. Sweat forced the torn dirt-stained white t-shirt I wore to cling to the protruding bones of my spine. I thirsted for a cold drink of water to soothe parched and cracked bleeding lips. On occasion, I dared to beg Dad for a break and his response came quick as always.

"Father, can we please stop for a drink?" I asked one blazing afternoon, daring to converse with him in any manner.

"Don't be such a baby. Keep working. Be a man. We need to finish." Jan Bednarz hurled the uncaring words at me.

I hung my head in defeat and went back to work, knowing any resistance to his orders would be detrimental to a healthy future. The dust swirled around the scythe, making a distinct slicing noise as I moved through the grass. The edge of the cutting knife was as sharp as the tongue of the man who controlled my world.

I think I must have been twelve years old when I first started making hay. Dad and I piled up the grass for several hours a day during the warm summer months until we had enough to feed the animals through the cold winter season. Some July and August days were unbearably hot, and we worked until our strength was gone. Life seemed insufferable to me as a defenseless child growing up a peasant farm boy in rural Poland in the 1920s and '30s.

My dad was strict with me especially since I was the oldest and a male child. I had to do most of the farm chores alone. Little did I know when the outdoor jobs I did on the farm were completed, my life would get even harder for me. I never had time to think past the present day I lived in and did not think anything would ever change. Oh, I was surely mistaken!

When our farm became a well-managed operation at the end of each day, and my siblings had grown old enough to help, I saw my life take an unexpected turn and not for the better. Dad decided the time was right to make me leave our home and go work for relatives. Aniela, Kasia, Bronia, and Stanley were getting old enough to do chores, and father no longer had to depend on me to keep the farm in good working order. He knew he could now put my younger sisters and brother to work, doing many of the jobs I had previously done on the farm.

At age twelve, my parents told me I would be leaving home to work for their relatives. I had no idea what jobs would be waiting for me or how long I would have to stay away from home. I found out soon enough.

Before I turned thirteen, my parents did send me away to work on a farm for people I did not know. There was no way I could have known the worst months of my life so far were about to begin. I have to believe my parents were unaware of what was in store for their firstborn son at the hands of evil kin, or perhaps they would have reconsidered their decision.

When I met my aunt and uncle, they had wickedness in their eyes toward me. I knew I was in trouble. They began shouting orders at me the minute I arrived on their farm.

"What are you looking at?" shouted the tall, thin angry man in the doorway of the farmhouse.

"Yeah, the cows need to be fed," echoed the large woman standing behind him.

I sauntered off, wondering where the cows were.

Before long, I found out these relatives of mine hated me for no reason. They didn't care whatsoever who I was or how I was feeling except that I came to work for them. They really did not know me at all and made no effort to find out anything. To them, I was just a slave boy coming to do their farmwork for the summer season.

When I started working for my relatives, I had never been away from home. Dad pushed me out of the house and made me walk several miles to my relative's farm. He told me I was being adopted out to my aunt and uncle for whatever they wanted me to do for them. I was sad to leave my mom and siblings. I felt lonely as soon as I left home.

The man at the farm was my mother's brother or an uncle of mine. He and his wife had no children. I think they were unable to have children. I am not really sure about the reason my aunt was barren. Anyway, they didn't have any kids to help them do chores on their farm. This is how my dad got the idea for them to give me a job for the summer and get rid of one mouth to feed. He always complained about not having enough food for the family! Now he was free of me and had no worry about the family starving.

Early on, the plan for me to work there was put in motion on a visit by these relatives to our farm during the spring season when my dad had expressed his fear to them that he did not know how he could afford to feed six children any longer.

"Our children are hungry and I cannot seem to put enough food on the table to satisfy them all," my dad complained to his brother-in-law.

Their faces lit up at the opportunity to hire their nephew for slave labor, and Dad knew he had struck gold. So on this one particularly fine morning, while they were sitting around our modest kitchen table, Dad and his in-laws made out a schedule for my life starting with the coming summer.

"Jozef seems to be a strong young man. Is he a hard worker?" my uncle inquired of my father.

"Oh, yes, and he can stay in the fields all day for you. He is worth a lot," Dad offered.

"I can take him off your hands if he will work hard for me," he declared as his wife, Patiele, smiled from the corner of the room as he spoke.

"Tell him what to do and he will do whatever you ask. I have taught him well." Dad was grooming them for a deal.

On that day, I peeked around the kitchen door and listened to the depressing conversation I was hearing. My fate had been sealed. I was on the way to becoming a slave child. Our relatives had quickly volunteered to take me off Dad's hands. This was the perfect solution for everyone, and I had no choice in the matter.

Dad told our relatives I could work for free if they gave me food to eat and a place to sleep. I know they were able to afford to hire help to work on their farm, but why pay someone when they could have me for no pay? The decision was an easy one for all of them.

On that day, my aunt and uncle agreed to take me without any hesitation. I was expected to live with them for the summer and possibly indefinitely. Dad promised my services to them in a couple weeks when I finished school and what he needed me to do for him on our farm.

Those next weeks passed way too fast. Before I knew what was happening, I had begun the excruciating long walk to my aunt and uncle's farm for what seemed like an eternity, only to be greeted by them in a snarly manner. My guts told me I was in for a rough ride.

I remember my uncle's wife name as Pateile. She was a very large woman who was not pretty. Her immediate rudeness gave me the excuse to refuse to call her a lady. She had no manners or kindness in her heart. She was scary looking with black stringy locks and facial hair. Her eyes were dark and threatening, and she reminded me of a witch who did not provide any kind of substitution for my wonderful mother. I saw no signs of affection from her toward me.

In my idea, Pateile and her husband were infertile probably because of her weight. Not having children to do their farmwork was definitely to their disadvantage with a large farm to tend. I believe the perfect answer to their problem had been predetermined by my dad. It didn't matter if I was only twelve years old. Nobody seemed to care what I wanted. Kids were not allowed an opinion about anything in Poland. When the time was right, Dad instructed me to grab a few clothes and leave our home for an undetermined number of days, months, or years.

My aunt and uncle lived on a big farm. With so many things to do to operate a successful farmstead, it was obvious they needed lots of help with the chores. I couldn't believe all the work needing to be done when I first saw the fields and the livestock. So I would help do their farmwork and take pressure off both families. When I first arrived, I wished I could have run away back home. At this point, I still had no idea what was in store for me.

I felt bad about leaving my family and doing someone else's farm chores. I knew I had to do what I was told for the good of everyone else in the two families. I prayed I would be able to return home soon. Somehow, things seemed to work out for me when I asked God for help. I continued to pray for courage and strength as usual.

Once on my aunt and uncle's farm, there seemed to be little I could do to change what was happening to me. In Poland, you did what you were told. If you didn't do what the adults made you do, you were beaten, starved, or worse. Reporting abuse of children was never heard of in this old country when I was a kid. Adults simply did what they felt like to children short of murder.

The day I arrived at my aunt and uncle's farm and walked off the porch in search of the cows, I could see lots of work needed to be done. A couple of beautiful, shiny-coated brown-haired horses stood elegantly, watching me pass by the corral heading toward the barn. Several head of cattle turned their necks away from the watering trough to gaze at the stranger walking on the other side of the silo. A couple pigs snorted in the mud near the barn as chickens raced around cackling in the sunlight. Were there more animals I hadn't seen? What was left?

I noticed wheat and bean crops peering through the dirt in the fields as I surveyed the panoramic view of the farm. A big beautiful garden waited to be tended and a large grove on their property contained numerous fruit trees. The farm owned by my relatives was bigger than any I had seen before in the district of Sambor. I guess you could say they were rich and I would be busy.

Once at the farm, I could see the chores would be endless. I soon found out life at my aunt and uncle's place would be rough after I heard the first orders barked at me. When the initial command came, a second one followed almost in unison.

"Jozef, once you are done watering the horses, pitch hay for them," my uncle ordered in a loud voice at me.

As soon as I set foot on the farm, I had to begin chores without being offered a drink or a rest for weary legs after the long walk to the final destination of my adoption. No rest for the innocent here!

"And when the work is done, you will bed down in the barn," Patiele scoffed at me as she walked rudely away. So the first of many nights spent on this farm I would I sleep in the barn.

Eventually, Patiele explained she wanted me to be ready to get up early in the morning and start working immediately. This was her excuse for making me sleep in the barn with the animals.

I had never slept on bad-smelling straw in cold damp air among animals and felt like one myself before I moved here. The brick agricultural farm building was where I laid my head at night from then on. The unkind relatives I worked for never offered me a warm bed as long as I remained on their farm.

Unfortunately for me, I overslept one morning, and my aunt came with a broomstick and a beating to wake me up.

"Get up, you lazy waif!" came her death-defying scream echoing through the dust-filled rafters.

Whack! The wood of the broom bruised the gentle skin on my backside and brought me to a quick awakening. At first, I was confused as to my whereabouts until I saw the ugly sneer on Patiele's face. What a sight to see first thing in the morning!

After that first lashing, I conspired to set a trap so I could be warned when my aunt was coming to beat me if I overslept. I placed a shovel in front of the barn door before I went to bed from then on and felt safe with a plan in action to defend myself against the evil witch. If anyone came into the barn early in the morning, I would wake up at the sound of the metal tool falling onto carefully placed horseshoes. However, I did not oversleep again!

Both my aunt and uncle treated me like I was a bum. Since they didn't have children of their own, they didn't really know what to do with a child. They were mean to me no matter how hard I worked for them. I was just their adopted slave kid. I meant nothing more to them.

My uncle was not a normal person. He bitched constantly. Nothing could ever be done exactly right for him. I pitched too much hay for the horses or missed an egg among the chickens or slopped the manure in the wrong place. The work I did turned out to be unsatisfactory to him on a daily basis.

One afternoon proved to be a painful reminder of my uncle's usual cruelty. During some repair work, he put a rock under the manure spreader and told me to hold the wheel, which I did.

"Now put your finger here," he said and pointed to a spot behind the spoke cylinder. I did as my uncle told me to do.

When I put my hand exactly where I was asked to, he ran over one of my fingers with the wheel.

"Ouch!" He pinched the finger so hard blood came to the surface of the skin and pressure built up under the nail. My whole hand throbbed and caused terrible pain in the fingers. For a kid like me, the pain was beyond belief.

My uncle ignored painful screams coming from me when he squished my finger with the manure machine. He had no sympathy for my agony and never apologized for hurting me.

"Stop whining!" he yelled. "This wouldn't have happened if you did what I told you to do!" Then he laughed at my discomfort.

"Maybe next time, you will be more careful," he continued to badger me.

I couldn't believe he made me feel like I deserved to be hurt. I wondered how long I would have to endure more torture at his hands.

My aunt and uncle were religious people, but my uncle had a little of the devil in him. He made me do things I did not know how to do and criticized me for doing jobs incorrectly. I milked the cows and brushed the horses. I fed the pigs. I walked the crop fields removing the weeds and crops grown from previous seeds of a different kind now in the field. I pitched hay for the horses. I worked night and day. I cleaned up the manure. Since it was summertime, I cleaned the wheat and beans in the fields. I pitched hay for the horses. I removed weeds and previous crops still in the fields. I worked night and day and did my best. Yet my uncle complained about everything I did.

"You are too slow," my uncle griped day after day.

Conditions did not improve for me over the months at the farm of my relatives. I was not complimented by my aunt and uncle for the good things I had done for them. They never said thank-you for any of the chores I finished every night. I did not receive any rewards for my hard work. Yet I refused to protest and did not venture to find out what they would have done if I had. Worst of all, I missed my mom and my brothers and sisters all the time. I feared I would never get to go home before I died on this disgusting, dirty farm.

Later on during my stay, I got into trouble at my aunt and uncle's farm with a gun I had hidden in the barn. The weapon was one I found in the forest when I was with a friend of mine shortly before coming to live there. At the end of WWI, guns could be found hidden under the brush in the forest. My friends and I found some of those guns and I kept one of the small shotguns. I felt safe having the weapon with me when I slept alone at night in the dark of the cold barn. I meant no harm to anyone with this piece of protection.

Guns were regulated by the authorities in Poland. When I was a young boy, the Russians came to rule Poland for a few months or so. One of their laws made possessing a gun illegal for the citizens of the Sambor district. When the Russians occupied Poland, the laws were strict against having guns. I knew I shouldn't have one, although I didn't care much about that particular law. I felt better having the piece and kept it well hidden, or so I thought. I was mistaken.

One day, Patiele came out into the yard and caught me admiring my treasure. She yelled at me to give the weapon to her. I knew she wouldn't give it back to me if I gave it to her. I refused to give up the gun and ran away in a hurry to disappear out of sight. Because she was so big, my aunt could hardly run fast enough to see where I went. I knew I could easily get away from her and hide my prize possession. So I did.

I ran to the barn as fast as my legs would carry me. I quickly found a shovel and lifted the dirt deep enough to conceal the gun in a hole before she could find me. When I accomplished my task, I moved to another part of the large cowshed.

When Patiele found me in the sleeping quarters of the stable, she didn't see where I had hidden the gun. She was extremely angry, and she would get me back, though unlike in the past when I had been punished by her many times for no specific reason. This time I would be deserving of being in actual trouble now that I had disobeyed her.

Oh my! There was fire in Patiele's eyes when she found me hiding up in the loft.

"Get down here, young man. Where is that gun?" she ordered me from the loft.

"What gun?" I lied. Oh no. Confession would be an appropriate choice for me again, although I had not been allowed to go to church or to the Confessional since I had arrived here.

Patiele was furious when I ran away from her and lied about the gun. I knew there would be consequences. I just wasn't sure what she would do to me this time.

What my aunt did do to me next was unthinkable for someone as young as I was. Madness overtook all her sensibility about the gun and she took me to the police and turned me in to the district of Sambor authorities. She probably thought if I kept the gun, I would shoot her for all the times I had been physically and verbally abused by her. I would not ever have used the gun against that woman, although she must have felt helpless around me with a gun in my possession in order for her to have gone to such extremes to get it away from me. I couldn't believe she had informed the police.

I was forced by my aunt to go to the police station in Brzesciany where she told them I had a gun and would not surrender the weapon to her. The police put me in a Polish squad car, most-likely a Peugeot 201. I was brought back to my aunt and uncle's farm where officers asked me to get the gun and give it to them. Having any kind of weapon at my age would not have been legal in those days.

"Give us the gun," the officer instructed gruffly.

With my body shaking nearly uncontrollably, I bravely denied I had a gun and refused to show anyone where I hid my weapon.

I was arrested on the farm in the barn when I refused to get the gun. An officer immediately handcuffed and shoved me into the back of the ancient police buggy, and I was hauled away back into town and put in jail.

The policeman in charge pointed his gun at my face and said, "If you try to escape, I shoot you!"

He was not kidding. I was no one to him.

Imagine the scene! At age twelve, I had to stay overnight in a cold, damp jail cell for not giving the police my gun. The experience was very frightening for a young boy like me. I was freezing and scared in the jail. I did not sleep with closed eyes, and there was no blanket for me to cover myself in order to be protected from the bugs and mice crawling on the floor. The jail was a terrible place to be. I just wanted to go home and be with my own family. I was tired of everyone's abusiveness.

The police released me the next morning to go back to my aunt and uncle. I had to walk a couple miles back to their farm. When I got there, I had to do my chores without any sleep or food. The only good thing to happen out of the whole incident was that no one ever found my gun, and Patiele never said another word to me about my treasure. I figure she must have thought the police had taken my weapon away, or I would not have been released.

Patiele made life very bad for me. I will tell you some things about my aunt Patiele. She was originally from the Ukraine. I think she must have weighed 250 to 300 pounds. She had something wrong with her personality. She was a mean person. I do not know what made her that way. I don't believe she was truly a religious person. Nothing good came from her.

One day, I merely walked by Patiele in the kitchen minding my own business on the way to the barn when she slapped me across the face for no reason. She hit me so hard she nearly knocked my teeth out. She stood there and laughed as I crouched in pain in front of her.

She had done it now. I could not take any more abuse from her. Inside myself, I decided I would not be at their farm anymore. I was very mad at both my aunt and my uncle. I no longer cared what my parents would do to me if I left this farm. No more Patiele or my uncle! I was done with both of them for good.

Immediately after the rude attack on me, I went to the barn and gathered the few belongings I had and hit the dusty road. I was going home!

I did leave my aunt and uncle's farm on that day. I walked to my parent's home feeling free and at peace. I never ever went back to their farm. I don't remember how long I worked there and it doesn't matter. At the time, I just wanted to go home. I walked ten to twelve kilometers back to my parent's farm hoping they would not force me to return to my previous hell. They did not.

This was a good day for me.

I told my dad what happened at our relative's farm, and I was so happy when he accepted me back home. He must have known his brother-in-law's wife was not a good person. He did let me stay home. God had granted a miracle.

CHAPTER FIVE

Russia Comes to Poland

A few months after I came home from my aunt and uncle's farm, I began to wonder how long my dad would let me stay. There were eight of us in the family living in the same small house when I returned. I was thirteen by this time. Many families in Brzesciany were suffering economically as were we. As usual, there wasn't much food for us to eat some days. We watched our neighbors struggle also, and I knew my time at home would be limited.

When I went home from my relative's farm, for a while at least, life in Poland seemed to be starting to get a little better. People were finding more chances for employment after WWI. This was a good thing.

Here are some things I remember about how Brzesciany and Sambor were before WWII changed everything. My village had about 1,200 people after WWI, compared to nearby Sambor with a 20,000 population. Half of the people of Sambor were Roman Catholic with the remaining residents being Jewish or other religions. The main enterprise in the district of Sambor involved the timber industry. Many people were hired for jobs in sawmills or in cutting wood for lumber. The next most prosperous occupations were farming, construction, and selling clothes.

I learned about Polish life from my Jewish friends when I did go back to school for a little while. The Jews controlled a lot of the enterprise in Poland except for the timber and logging which the government controlled. Jews were in control of much of the prosperity of Poland, as I remember. This became a problem for them. Both the Russians and Germans wanted what the Jews had. In particular, the German officials, especially Adolf Hitler, felt the Jewish people in business had too much control of the enterprise in my country. Eventually, he would vow to change their power and riches. This is my own philosophy about what happened in Poland before WWII.

In September of 1939, when I was at the age of fifteen, the Russians moved into eastern Poland and entered Brzesciany. Their occupation in my country lasted until June of 1941.

With Russia in control of Poland, all children were forced to go to school to learn how to speak the Russian language. This new government wanted Polish students to be able to communicate with them and learn Russian propaganda. Understandably, if we didn't learn about our own country, we would not be able to comprehend the politics. This was a plan strictly for the advantage of a country not all that foreign to us all. Polish education had previously been bilingual and my Russian language education came in handy during wartime when I met other Russians I needed to be able to communicate with.

The Russian loggers hired me to work in the forests when I was fifteen. Before they came, the forests were considered sacred. Trees were not allowed to be cut down. These government workers changed all that. They raided the forests of all the good timber and sent the wood back to Russia for their own use. The wood from the Polish forests was like gold to them.

I helped to cut down the huge trees in the forest. The saws were so big it took four men to use the saw to cut a tree in half. There were two guys on either side of the saw constantly pushing against the other side in order to slice this wood. The process took a long time and the work was extremely exhausting. We sawed from sun up until sun down. It took all day to cut some of the historic giant wood down because the trees were very old and big. Can you believe I was only fifteen doing this hard work?

The job I had in the forest turned out to have to be done during the winter months. Temperatures were twenty to thirty degrees below zero sometimes! Oh, yeah! I was certainly a tough young man working in extreme cold weather conditions.

I worked in the forest for many hours all day long. At night, I stayed in the nearby villages with the townspeople. By the age of sixteen, I was still cutting wood during the day and sleeping on straw on the floor with the other workers at night. The townspeople were poor and they had no rugs for us to sleep on, so we slept on the straw. The accommodations were not comfortable, but I was too tired to care most nights.

When we were allowed to take a break and have some time to eat, I had to find food for myself. Most of the workers had to buy the bread the Russians provided, but I had my own. I brought bread from home to eat when Mom had enough to give me a loaf and I was close enough to get some. I didn't trust the Russian's food. They would give the rotten stuff to the workers, and I feared I would get sick if I ate it.

We stayed for two weeks at a time working in a certain forest. This was the limit. The days we worked in a place were counted. The country officials gave the order for us to leave after the allowed number of days was up. If we didn't go and leave the forest in two weeks, that would cause a petition against the workers. Then the Russians would come and get us and ship us to Siberia. Siberia meant death! Definitely, we would move to a different forest after two weeks. Obeying the law had to be a priority.

I got paid to work in the forest. When I brought the money home, my dad asked me if I got paid.

"Jozef, where is the money they paid you?" Dad would jump me as soon as I came home.

I gave the money to Mom right away when I arrived at our farm.

I told Dad I had already given it to Mom knowing he would take my money unless it were hidden or given immediately to her. If I would give the cash I earned to my dad, he would just use it to buy booze. He drank liquor whenever he could find a way to buy some even if our family was hungry and needed the money for food. His drinking was an especially hard thing for my mom. She was just trying to keep everyone from starving.

When the Russians emptied the forest of valuable wood, and I could no longer find work there, I went back home only to hear father constantly telling me that he and my mother could not afford to feed six children and themselves. In those days, it was more important to my dad that I had a job rather than go to school. I never returned to complete my education after I finished the eighth grade because I was working. What I did learn up until I was fourteen did serve me well throughout my life. I was expected to find another job after I was no longer needed in the forest.

My father's words came quickly after I arrived home from the forest. "Jozef, you must leave and go find work," he ordered.

Out of respect for him and afraid of what I might say, I remained speechless.

"There is not enough food for us all. Go to town and find something to do. Bring us back the money to buy the food we need!" my dad yelled loudly and chased me out of the house as soon as I became comfortable on the farm again. I tried to resist.

"Father, please don't make me leave. I have never been to town alone to work. I have cleaned up the grove and repaired the broken machinery. I can raise more crops." I fought back by showing him what I had accomplished on the farm and how proud I was of myself.

"Go!" He still made me leave. There could never be a compromise with him.

So I gathered a few clothes, wrapped them in a handkerchief bag, and off I went back to town.

CHAPTER SIX

A Job in the Bakery

My dad was strict and unyielding to me. I had been sixteen years old for a couple months when he forced me to leave home for the third time. I hugged mom and my younger siblings, said a final goodbye, and headed out toward town to look for work.

I had to walk the four long miles to town not knowing where I would go this time for sure. When I left, the day was young so I could get to town before dark and find a place to sleep. As I remember, spring was coming when I strolled into town—not a bad time of year to look for a new job!

I knew I wanted to work in the bakery, so I went in the direction of a bread shop I knew of in Brzesciany. Once again, I missed Mom and my brothers and sisters when I left. I knew I must forget about the sorrow I felt in my heart. No matter how bad my situation seemed to be, this was what I had to do. I always wanted to try to be a baker anyway.

When I arrived at the bakery in Brzesciany, I was very tired. I snuck into the barn behind the bakery where the owners kept their hogs. I climbed up the ladder and slept above the noisy animals. When I woke up, I retrieved the leftover bread the owners threw in the building to feed the hungry pigs and went back where I had taken the well-deserved nap to eat my treasure.

With my hunger satisfied, I waited up in the loft trying to decide what to do next. I fell back asleep after a short while.

I had been sleeping for a couple hours when a loud bang woke me up. The owner's son kicked at my boots. I had been found and now was afraid of what he would do to me. I could tell by his uniform he was a lieutenant in the Polish army.

Surprisingly, he asked me, "Do you want to go to work, young man?"

I replied to him, "Sure, sir." I knew this would be my favorite job.

"Well then, come on. That is enough sleeping for you. There is work to be done in the bakery." The handsome Polish soldier scolded me.

"Yes, sir." I saluted the stately soldier and followed him into the shop.

I remember the name of the bakery was Wrzask. I even recall the name of the street the bakery to be Przemyska.

I liked my new job from the first day the generous soldier offered me employment. His parents, the owners, were nice to me and the smell of the bread was heavenly. I knew I was right where I wanted to be if I had to help support my family.

My job at the bakery was delivery of the breads they baked. They had me deliver the freshly baked bread to the customers in the city of Brzesciany from the basket of a two-wheeled bicycle. I used a white sheet to cover the bread and keep it clean and fresh.

I delivered bread all day long after the bakers were done baking the daily orders. By the end of the day, I was exhausted. Sometimes, I would stop my bike and take a rest and just fall asleep. I was lucky when one of the townspeople would come along and wake me up so I wouldn't get into trouble with the boss.

I started my day out at the bakery early in the morning. I usually had only three hours of sleep at night. In order to prepare everything for the bakers in the morning, I had to get to the bakery before they arrived. I was very busy. There was a lot to do. I had to prepare the dough for dark and white bread.

Even though the work was hard, I wanted to be a baker myself. Bakers had to be certified in Poland, and becoming a baker was a complicated process. I knew this process would take me a long time. I was willing to work long and hard to make my dream come true.

At night, I slept upstairs in the hog house behind the bakery. The owners kept the hogs for their food and to sell for butchering. All the old bread from the bakery went out to feed them. Nothing went to waste in Poland. When the hogs were big enough, they were butchered. After the meat was processed, some of the pork was sold at the market and the rest they kept to eat for themselves. In Poland, having fresh meat to eat was a luxury.

Sleeping above the hogs at night was not the best way for me to sleep. There were lots of rats in the barn. I could always hear them running around during the night. Remember, my age was sixteen! This wasn't a pleasant living situation for a teenager by himself at such a young age. I don't mean to complain about my life. I loved to work in the bakery. There were unpleasant things I had to put up with which didn't seem fair at my age. I guess what I missed most of all was the time I should have been allowed to spend growing up with my brothers and sisters. I came to realize life happened not always as one planned or dreamed about.

Mine was a tough life from the beginning. Almost from my childhood years onward. Work. Work. Work. I even worked on Sundays at the bakery. I was not a baby like kids are today. I didn't want my own kids to have a life like mine, but I did expect them to work hard and do some chores. My story is not so usual a one for kids to understand!

My mom would come to town to the bakery to see me once in a while. She made me so happy when she came to the bakery. I did miss her a lot.

When Mom came to the bakery, I would take the money I made and give it to her. She would smile at me and she did not smile often. The times I gave her the money I made she was happy knowing it would make life better for our family. Of course, she was glad to see me also.

When I delivered the bread to the customers at Christmas-time, I received lots of gifts. At each store where I delivered bread, the people would give me holiday gifts. I received handmade mittens, scarves, and hats and other nice presents.

Most of my customers in the city knew who I was. They were nice to me. I got money for Christmas from some of them. They gave me gifts on Easter and other holidays also. Easter was as big a holiday in Poland like Christmas was. These were special occasions for me when working in the bakery!

Sometimes, Dad would come to town also. He would see all the special presents I got from the customers and he would want them. I gave my mom the gifts and not to my dad. Instead, I gave him fresh bread from the bakery. I told my boss I gave my dad some bread. He said it was OK. My mom was happy to get the gifts, and my dad did like the bread.

My dream for a job was always to learn how to be a baker. In Poland, it would take me four years to become a certified baker. I never got the chance. All my hard work went for nothing in the bakery because of the Soviet invasion of Poland and the Second World War. I knew in the future I would like to become a baker and make good wages. Sadly, I never did.

I did not get normal pay for working in the bakery since I was not a certified baker. The owners of the bakery did not have to pay me; however, my employers fed me and gave me a place to sleep. I did get some money and gifts from the customers, which made all the difference for my hard work.

While I worked in the bakery, the events occurring in the world were oblivious to me. People talked on the street about the Germans coming to take over Poland and they talked of a man named Hitler. At the time, I did not know who he was. Soon, I would come to know this hateful person, and over the next year, I would find out about the coming war.

Eventually after the war started with Poland, German Nazis moved into eastern Poland in 1941 and took over everything. They wanted all the most important and expensive possessions the Poles had. Jews were not allowed to operate businesses so most were closed. Then the local Jewish people began to disappear. The Germans were putting them in ghetto prisons in Warsaw and other places. Poland was under attack in every way possible.

After moving into Brzesciany, German soldiers came to the bakery where I worked. They made everyone in the shop leave the premises. The owners were forced to give up their business or die. Rather than sacrifice their lives, my good friends left the precious professional trade they had built up and allowed the Germans to take control of their baking company.

I wanted to stay and work at the bakeshop. As a young and naïve teenager, I didn't understand what was happening with the soldiers. I asked the Germans if I could remain there and work in the bakery. A soldier came after me and yelled some words in the German language. He pointed a gun at me, and I was chased out of bakery forever.

Russians, who previously controlled the eastern part of the country, left Poland on June 29, 1941. On July 1, 1941, the Germans moved in. Sadly, I left the bakery the day the German soldiers came and kicked me out. I walked back home to my parent's farm with mixed feelings. I was happy to go home, yet I had a bad sense about what would happen next.

CHAPTER SEVEN

Russia and Germany Invade Poland

After I got home from the bakery, everything started to change for Poland. In August of 1939, prior to WWII, the German-Soviet Pact was formed, part of which forbade war between the countries. However, the agreement allowed Germany to attack Poland without fear of Russian interference. On September 1, 1939, Germany invaded Western Poland and WWII began. A couple weeks later, the Soviet Union sent troops into the eastern part of the country, including Brzesciany and the surrounding areas.

Later on, Hitler broke the pact and German soldiers moved through Poland and invaded the Soviet Union in June of 1941, causing the Russians to leave my country. Just days after Russian soldiers left Poland, the Nazis came to Brzesciany!

During Germany's second occupation of my country, Hitler's German Nazis infiltrated all of Poland. They continued to move to the west after Warsaw surrendered to them in September of 1939. After destroying all routes of transportation: airports, bus stations, and bridges, the Nazis controlled all polish lands for the next two years. Nazi Germany would maintain control of Poland until January of 1945, after the defeat of Hitler. After WWII, Polish borders changed and Soviet troops occupied Poland along with most of Eastern Europe. Brzescany actually disappeared off the map after WWll.

When the Nazi's overran Poland, rumors circulated of how they had seized whatever possessions Poles owned of any value. The Jewish people were primarily targeted and moved forcefully into ghettos in

Warsaw as the result of the proposed ethnic cleansing of the country. Hitler intended to destroy Poland completely and expand living space for Germany according to his documented plans. News of the seizure of Jews and their belongings as well as executions of high ranking Polish officials and other important individuals travelled quickly from town to town. Fear crippled everyone. It appeared no one was safe, especially when non-Jewish people also began to disappear or to be taken by force from their homes for slave labor.

Polish lands were rich with grain before WWII. Rice and rye were abundant in my country. The Germans took most the grain away and left us little to nothing. Our Polish army had been quickly been defeated at the onset of the war, and the people were defenseless for the most part. My people were losing everything they had to the Nazis, including their lives.

When the war broke out in Poland and later throughout Europe, Nazi soldiers went into homes and took strong men to work in their ammunition factories and on farms for the Reich in Germany. Polish Catholics were the primary target for forced labor who were banished from their homes and families. No one dare refuse to go with them. The Nazis killed anyone who did not obey their orders without question. The ruthless ways of the soldiers had already been demonstrated by them in the treatment of Jews who had been corralled from their homes and taken to Warsaw and put into the established Ghetto or murdered for refusal to leave or for attempts to escape. No one really knew what was going to happen to the Jews or why the Germans were stealing all their wealth and forcing them to leave their homes. Most were loaded like cows would have been onto trucks or into trains to an unknown fate and little did anyone know of the seriousness of their situation. The murderous nightmare for Poland began in 1939 and continued on until 1945 at which time Joseph Stalin made life in Poland much worse. I believe he murdered over 68 million Jews and other Poles-more than Hitler did. He was a terrible man whose influence kept Poles under Communist rule until 1990.

The German soldiers were hungry for food and valuables. They stole whatever they wanted from my people. If anyone tried to resist, the Nazis riddled their bodies with bullets until they died. Their persecution weakened my people day by day. The torture and senseless murders of the Poles was inhumane and appeared unstoppable.

The war was in full force before long, and Poland was no match for the Nazis. The country I loved became the first battleground of WWII in 1939. Everyone was affected, however, my own worst fate was yet to come.

Our family received word that one of my cousins had been murdered by the Nazi's sometime after the war began. I was sixteen at this time and considered heading out into the countryside to join the Polish locals who were trying to save people as rumors of impulsive murders by the Nazis abundantly circulated. No one crossed these soldiers, and if I had joined the Polish Underground, and was caught by the Nazi's, the lives of my family would have been placed in danger. I felt I couldn't take the chance of risking any family member's safety, so I stayed home to help protect them as long as possible. Truthfully, I felt pretty helpless.

Late in 1939, negative propaganda had spread across Poland about Hitler and his evil plans to eradicate Jews. When in town, I heard whisperings indicating a secret underground resistance planned to form against the Germans invading my country. By 1940, some of my friends joined this secretive organization called the Polish Underground. Their mission was to attempt to stop the Nazis from taking native Jewish people to be imprisoned in the Warsaw Ghetto or worse. Many local men were hopping on board to join the fight against what we now call the Holocaust.

A best friend of mine in Poland belonged to the Polish Underground. His and other stories of courage and bravery are unbelievable. My friend's name is Stanislaw Zirkovsky. Stan survived the war and currently lives in Czestochowa, Poland. He assisted in sabotaging trains carrying Jews to extermination camps in Poland. During one raid, Nazi soldiers intercepted a raid and beat Stanley nearly to death. His neck was broken, and his genitals were injured, rending him unable to father children. Consequently, he survived the war but never married. Instead of taking a wife, he became a successful businessman in Klodzko, Poland, making and selling leather belts and purses. (I visited him there in his private shop on my visits to Poland until he moved to Czestochowa and retired in his eighties, where this true hero of the war lives a modest quiet life in retirement and now is in his nineties.)

In spite of suffering serious injuries from the war while working with the Polish Underground, Stan verbalized to me his happiness some Jews did escape with him the nights he helped sabotage the trains filled with Jews destined for certain death. He has done good things in his life. Luckily, he survived his injuries and escaped from the Nazis. I cannot imagine those soldiers knew he was Jewish or he would have been shot for sure.

Stan and I are the same age. We are still best friends and we correspond regularly to each other. I have visited him every time I went to Poland. Since the war, he has had a good life for himself even being in Poland all these years and not being married. Our different religious beliefs have not made a difference in our close friendship.

Stan taught me many things about the Polish Underground over the years when I visited with him in Poland. He told me they were also known as the Polish Secret State. The organization was a powerful underground resistance group in Poland especially during WWII. There were both military and civilian members who fought for the economic, political, and religious freedom of Poland among other reasons. One to two hundred thousand people were involved in this organization quietly supported by nearly all Polish citizens. The Polish Underground was the largest and most effective civilian resistance against the Nazi occupation in all of Europe during WWII. Stanley prided himself in having been a part of this life-saving organization.

According to Stan, the Polish Underground supplied intelligence to anti-Nazi military forces and particularly the British. This group saved more Jews than any other service organization during WWII. Of great importance to their cause, they disrupted German supply lines to the Eastern Front of WWII. People who were part of the Polish Underground were both rewarded and put in great danger during their service. I remember desperately wanting to help my country and join this organization again when I was seventeen, but the risk to my family was too great. So I continued to work on the farm and help support our family the best I could for as long as I was able and no one bothered us for several months.

CHAPTER EIGHT

Taken By Nazis

Nazi soldiers came to my parent's door on a sunny day in October of 1941. I was seventeen years old when they stomped loudly up the old worn wooden porch steps of our home and gruffly greeted my father when he opened the door. The Swastika patches on the shoulders of their uniforms reflected with a cold chill like a knife penetrating the bright sunlight and generating a nauseating sickness in the pit of my stomach as I peered around my father's shaking body. Fear gripped us both. The peaceful existence we had been enjoying recently appeared to be over.

Our family stood in fear at the sight of the angry looking men in uniform occupying the living room of the modest space we called home. No one knew for sure what they were after. As far as we could understand, the soldiers were yelling in their foreign language about wanting to take my dad, who was not a healthy man, with them. They had apparently intended to force him to go to Germany and work in a factory to make ammunition for the war in progress. The soldiers relayed they were following Hitler's orders. Resistance was obviously not an option by their tone of voice.

When the men reached for Dad's arm to take him, I spoke up.

"Take me. I substitute for my dad." I told the official looking men in dark gray uniforms in clear Polish words they seemed to understand.

The stoic Nazi soldiers glanced at me in disbelief and accepted my offer. They could probably see my dad would not be of much help to them.

I went with those frightening and unfamiliar Nazi soldiers on a sunny yet dark gloomy day in October of 1941 in order to save my father from a fate he would likely not survive. Before I left the house, I turned in gratitude toward my mother for all she had done for me. I explored her loving face and treasured the memory I would carry with me wherever I went, not knowing for how long a time it would be before or if I would ever see her smile again. I held back the tears and scanned the room for a final glance at the puzzled faces of my siblings: Aniela, Kasia, Stanley, Bronia, and Matteas. I never set eyes on my dad as I was about to leave for he had disappeared from sight, and I did not see him ever again after that day.

As I exited our home, Mom was visibly upset. She cried and cried (quietly, of course) as I left. I'm sure she didn't think she would ever see her first born son again. My mother as well as the rest of the family could do absolutely nothing to help me if they wanted to live. If anyone tried to stop the Nazi soldiers from taking what they wanted, we all would have been shot. Then all of us would be dead, and what was the sense of that? I had to go to Germany to do what Hitler had asked of Catholics like me or die. Mom knew she had to let me go.

I surrendered my free will to those Nazis in fear and out of respect for my dad in order to save the family from certain execution. At least everyone else in the house would be safe for now. And the Nazis were satisfied with their acquisition. Silently, I closed the door behind me with an indescribable ache in my heart and then I was gone.

I left my birth family and the normal existence I knew in Poland to go with Hitler's Nazi German soldiers on that sad day in October, 1941, instead of letting them take my father. Nothing in life would ever be the same for me. After this day, I would not see any of my family members for another twenty-three years. When I did see all of them years later, they had been relocated from southeast to southwest Poland. My beloved Brzesciany, where I was born and lived nearly eighteen years of life, would have been claimed by the Soviet Union and become a part of Ukraine after the war. As long as I have lived and traveled to Europe, I have not seen Brzesciany again after this day.

(Author's note: I have a strong opinion about this incident, knowing the things my father told me about his dad. I believe my father was probably forced by his own dad to go with the Nazi soldiers instead of going by himself. In my mind, I can see my grandpa pushing Dad toward the soldiers in order to save his own skin.)

As I rode the rusty old train to Hamburg, Germany, now a prisoner of the Nazi soldiers, I began to learn about Hitler from other captives in the same predicament as me. Today, I have my own ideas about who Hitler was and the kind of man he came to be. Back then, I was very innocent and knew little of him. Now I have learned much about his ways through my years in the war. I will like to tell some of what I think about him and his psychology.

Hitler's idea for the world was to create a superior race. He imagined himself being the leader of the world, allowing only perfect people to exist. I could never figure this one out for he was not even good-looking himself! However, in order to accomplish this goal, first he had to get rid of those people who didn't fit into his plan! Hitler's dream of perfect ethnicity and world domination would eventually cost many their lives.

Hitler's ideas did not correspond to his own religion. I had heard that he was born a Catholic. His religious roots never prevented him from turning devilish. I believe many people can turn evil even if they are well-educated or religious. Hitler had bad blood in him as well as the power to turn other people murderous.

At first, the common people of Germany trusted Hitler. They believed he would be the savior of Germany. What fools those people were! Ekland boosted Hitler's self-confidence until the man actually believed he was destined to have Germany for himself as some say was forecasted by his birth chart years before. Hitler was described and called *Fuhrer* by the woman who did this chart prospecting his life's journey. Later on, many addressed him as *Fuhrer*, which meant leader.

I have been told Hitler's birth chart is said to contain chilling and amazing prophesies about his life. He believed he would rise up to have great prominence in the world. I find the way people followed after him to be puzzling. Hitler was a fearful person, and because of his evilness during WWII, he has been called the second antichrist—next to Napoleon—who has been called the first. He might have destroyed the world if he had not been defeated.

I will never forget Hitler's face or the sound of his voice ringing in my ears demanding all to pay him homage and bow to the German government. He was a devil to me.

I believe Hitler to be similar to a natural preacher when he first came to Germany. You know I heard a story he actually studied for a while to be a priest? People in Poland talked of this unusual story. Catholicism would never have worked for him. His speeches were built up with hatred, and as time went on, religion of any kind was forbidden in Germany where he ruled.

Before WWII, Hitler promised a better life for Germans, and people were drawn to him by the emotions he stirred up in them. He made the citizens of Germany feel good about him and better about the future of their country. And his plan worked when the people elected him chancellor of Germany before the war in 1933! The lives of the German people deteriorated from then on.

After he ignored Germany's pact with Stalin, Hitler led the defeat of Russian forces in Germany and Poland. When the war began in 1939, he favored totalitarianism. You know he actually wanted to rule the world? Crazy! Crazy!

The operation of industries in Germany needed to support the war affected the entire country of Poland in many ways. The Nazis took up arms against the citizens of Poland, and the whole life of the country changed. Hitler needed men for his workforce, and Poland provided a solution to where he would obtain help as well as aid in his determination to break my country both morally and materially as a warning to all other European countries to follow his orders. Poland became Hitler's example to the world of how he would rule everyone.

In order to stop any kind of further learning, Hitler ordered all books be burned in Poland. Thousands of books were destroyed, affecting all aspects of passing on information from history to religion as he would not tolerate religion in any form. Of his eradicating all books in such a final way, some have said that they who start by burning books will end by burning men. How right they were!

And burn men he did. Hitler took Jewish Poles by force and imprisoned them. There was the Jewish question. What to do with them? At first, he poisoned the mentally impaired with gas and progressed his plan when Jews were annihilated with gas starting in December 1941 and later incinerated.

Chelmno, in rural Poland, became the first death camp where eventually primarily Jewish prisoners were burned alive. Many other facilities were quickly established in quiet remote areas near railways for easy access. I came to understand later on after being a POW the mass killings of innocent Poles and others had continued for nearly three years with an estimated three million deaths. My heart cries for the people of my country who died in such a savage way. It hurts me to even think about their pain before being gassed or burned to death.

I don't know how those men could do such horrible things to my people. It is a mystery to me. I find this incomprehensible someone would put a human being in an oven and burn them alive. I heard the Nazis took whole families with children and babies and little kids. Special facilities were built in Poland and Germany to cremate the bodies, so soldiers did not have to bury them. People told me prisoners had to do degrading jobs in the camps before they themselves were led to the extermination chambers. Male Jewish prisoners were humiliated by making them walk naked around the camps to see which ones were weak or sick. These would be the first to die along with the women and children who were not considered able to do jobs in the work camps. I know these things were true when prisoners in the concentration camps and people in Poland after the war talked about it. There is much we do not even know about yet!

Hitler's barbaric treatment of the Polish people was beyond my comprehension. He killed a friend of mine who was the same age as me. Soldiers took and killed him for no reason. I had a lot of fun with him when I was a boy. How can a seventeen-year-old understand such hatred? I wondered if I would end up the same way as I walked the last few steps on familiar gravel to another new challenge in my short life.

The Nazi soldiers pushed me into the back of an old dilapidated truck after we left my parent's house. I realized I had no other option than to go with Hitler's men. This I knew. If I refused, I would have been killed, and I was too young to die.

As I traveled with the soldiers and other prisoners, first in a smelly old jalopy truck and then on a ripped up steam train to Germany, I thought about many Jews I had known in my life. I remembered going to town with Dad when I was young and meeting some of the local Jewish businessmen. Some years later, those people I met would give me small jobs to do. Sometimes, I went into their stores to get the Kvass soda pop, like Coca-Cola, and would stay to sell the soft drinks for them at about ten cents (American money equivalent) to the people who came to town. When I sold ten bottles of soda, I got a few pennies back from the Jews to keep for the hard work I did for them.

The Jewish people came from all over Brzesciany to buy the eggs, milk, butter, and chickens Dad and I brought into town to sell from the farm. Their money helped my family to survive. I had no problems with those Jews! I didn't understand why there had to be a war over them.

Now I was leaving my mom as a prisoner of war. It wasn't her fault. We were both sad and afraid when I left. I was very afraid. I tried not to think about what would happen to me next. I prayed to God. I prayed a lot. I prayed hard. I needed God now more than I ever had in my life.

CHAPTER NINE

Transported to Germany

Life in the land of Polish peasants ruled by Poland and various countries over the centuries was already difficult when Hitler marched across Europe. Germany was struggling to establish its authority in that particular corner of the globe, and her war machine ran short of the manpower needed to fuel the effort. During the long trip to Germany, first by truck, then by train, I traveled with many other local prisoners to Berlin as part of the new workforce being taken forcefully from their native homes in order to accomplish a victory for Hitler. I call us prisoners because we were all kidnapped by the Nazis and guarded by German soldiers with machine guns on the journey to work camps. An attempt by of any us to escape would have been suicidal. We were trapped! At this point, the life we had known in Poland was over for us all.

As I watched the beloved country I had known since birth disappear before my eyes, I wondered what would become of me. I held on to a lifelong faith in God and continued to pray as I had previously done every morning. I asked the Lord to protect me and the precious family I left behind in Poland. When I started to feel sorry about the situation I was in and my heart ached with sadness, I would force myself to stop feeling hopeless before I broke down for good and put my life in danger. And I prayed!

The train ride across Poland and Eastern Germany became bumpy and uncomfortable. The conditions were poor on the train and a couple of men died from starvation and other medical problems during the trip. I heard of the deaths of prisoners as a result of dehydration and some from heat exhaustion during the summer transports. Fortunately for me, I traveled in the fall when temperatures were mild. I presumed some men may have frozen to death on the trains during the winter months also as there was no heat in the drafty cars.

The crowded, smelly train ride became just the beginning of the torture I assumed I would have to endure as a POW. I did force myself to tolerate the heat, the cold, the lack of food and water. I wondered if my dad would be surprised to see how well he had unknowingly groomed me for the miserable situation I had fallen into. Fear of what the future held threatened to throw me into an unescapable panic.

On the long ride to an unknown fate, the only positive part of the experience for me so far had been the ability to watch the beautiful scenery of the country I loved dance before my eyes. I treasured Poland, yet I still dreamed of America and freedom from the political prejudice and the social injustice I had seen here. Daydreaming of a new life in the United States gave me something to hold onto during the seemingly hopeless hours of bouncing uncomfortably in the train on my way to work for a war endeavor I wanted no part of. I feared for the lives of my family and tried not to think of the bad things that could happen to us all.

Instead of panicking over my situation, I solemnly enjoyed studying the rolling green hills of southern Poland. When I could get close enough to a window, I breathed the sweet country air into pollution-filled lungs and cleared my sinuses of the pungent smell of body fluids enveloping me. For a few brief moments now and then, I escaped my miserable prison.

There were many hours to think about what being a prisoner would mean for me while the train rolled noisily on to its final destination. Germany would be a strange place for me to be. I knew nothing of the country other than Hitler was there and the war was going on. I already missed my family. Although I had been away from home before, being away from them in the past I feared would not compare to what I would probably be facing in this foreign land if all the rumors I had heard were true. Speculating on how long I might be a prisoner in this foreign land seemed fruitless. Nothing was for certain anymore!

The stories I had heard about Adolf Hitler on the train were frightening me. I tried to ignore what was being said by others after we passed into Germany. I guessed we were getting close to the end of our journey by the road signs I saw. I tried to stay calm knowing my unearned prison sentence would soon begin. I found the situation I was in easier to bear by not thinking about what might happen next, helping me to keep some sense of mental stability. Dreams of going to America and fishing on a beautiful sunny day made the dark days ahead seem lighter and were a feeble attempt to hold on to my sanity.

When we arrived in Berlin, I took note of the enormous beautiful city. Large brick churches of Gothic design passed by my eyes. People strolled carefree on the city streets. Double-decked buses carried workers to their jobs. Office buildings several stories high lined some of the roads. Obvious evidence of the war was absent from this part of the city.

When we arrived at a military-type location, the Nazi soldiers unloaded us from the outdated train ride like cattle. We were pushed into a large unfriendly steel building and lined up for physical examinations with instructions to take off our clothes. The surroundings were cold and gloomy. I cannot put into words how frightened I was at this time.

Several of Hitler's puppets strip searched me and all POWs who came from the train. They put their hands in every hole in our bodies. I attempted to stand proud and act unaffected by their probing fingers. The worst humiliation of my life had just begun.

Oh dear God! I had never been touched by another person in such an offensive manner. Shame filled my being, however, I refused to show the embarrassment I felt to anyone. They could touch my body but not my soul!

When the soldiers were done groping our bodies, we were moved into another room. They sprayed us with horrible smelling chemicals to kill any lice we might have caught from other POW passengers on the train. Once the evil Nazi officials were satisfied we were bug free, they sent us to the showers in another room and the nightmare continued.

I showered naked along with all the other POWs and the degradation seemed to never end. Nazi soldiers laughed at us as we stood under the freezing water—our modesty stolen from us. Remember, I was seventeen! My previous life experiences had not prepared me for this awful and perverse treatment. I turned a heavy head away from everyone in shame as warm wet tears slid down my young innocent face unnoticed. I promised myself I would never let my captors see a drop of water come from these eyes after this day.

The Nazi soldiers were rough and mean. I experienced a new lower level of self-esteem when they inspected my body and gave their approval for me to work in the labor camp. I thought I was in hell as I was shoved here and there for the pleasure of the soldiers. One could only imagine what would happen next during the coming days, months, and possibly years of the war to follow. It felt as if the work of the devil surrounded me as I prayed for my life to be spared from a painful tragic death.

The Nazi soldiers fumigated us once more after our showers to make sure we didn't have any diseases we might spread to them or to each other. The last humiliation we endured before we were allowed to dress was to be completely shaved of all hair from our bodies. I could not even begin to comprehend the purpose of this last insult to my innocent body.

When the Gestapo (the Nazi police) was done spraying the putrid liquid on all of us held captive, they took the POWs who passed inspection to the Nazi work office and separated us into different groups. We were sent to various concentration camps and eventually labor camps in different parts of Germany. The concentration camps provided sleeping quarters and some working options while labor camps were anything from ammunition factories to farms. Not comprehending what was about to transpire, I struggled to remain strong and to answer my superiors politely as they led me away to a waiting military transport vehicle.

Here is the story of my imprisonment. My name is Jozef Bednarz. I became a prisoner of the Nazis during WWII. I was forcefully taken from my home and the family I love and moved to a foreign country to perform slave labor for a cause I do not understand. My body has been stripped, prodded, poked, searched, beaten, and sprayed with awful scents by people I would never let touch me under normal circumstances. A rugged old army truck has taken me and a group of other POWs to a place called a concentration camp in Hamburg, Germany. Nazi officials issued me a gray uniform coat to wear with a band bearing a P on the sleeve to tell the world I am no longer free human being. I am a Polish POW.

From this day on, my own fate would be up to me to some degree. I knew I had to save myself by staying healthy and being strong. The Nazis cared nothing about me or the personal welfare of any POW. They did plan to kill me and as many others as possible by starvation and strenuous labor. When I am dead, another POW would be put in my place and the cycle of abuse and death will continue. Knowing this was the plan, I am determined these evil men won't break me! I shall pray to God every day and survive.

CHAPTER TEN

Hamburg-Altona

After being thoroughly inspected physically in Berlin, I was sent to a concentration camp in Hamburg where I would spend my nights. A supporter of the Nazi Party by the name of Henry Jansen chose me with a group of other POWs to work for him during the day in Altona, a suburb of Hamburg. Henry was a German businessman forced to support Hitler in the war effort and be in charge of coal supplies needed for wartime industries. His coal operation was located in Altona, an important seaport city adjacent to Hamburg where coal arrived by ship several times a month. The black gold came to Henry's warehouses in trucks loaded from the gondolas at the seaport entrance. The coal transport vehicles were unloaded by slave laborers like me and stored-the priceless source of fuel for use in the war machine factories. As the manager of the crucial energy supply, Henry became my boss during the day, and at night, I was guarded by the Gestapo in the sleeping quarters of the concentration camp.

Before I was sent to work for Henry, the Nazi soldiers placed me along with other POWs in an old Presbyterian church converted into a concentration camp for forced labor workers in Hamburg. The address of the camp was 129 Dorothen Street, Wandsback, Hamburg, which held eighty older men who worked in forced labor camps throughout the area. I traveled from this artificial barracks to work every day with a special permit from the Nazi authorities. The location of my job site was not located in one of the normal places most POWs had been sent. Each morning I walked from my nightly primitive corridors to a certain corner location to get on a sidecar where I was taken to a warehouse for the day. At night, I returned to the dingy cold camp after working for Henry during daylight hours.

When I first arrived at the old church camp, the SS (Schutzstaffel, the Nazi protection squadron) and the Gestapo (the Nazi State Secret Police formed by Herman Goring) informed new POWs we would all be monitored during our sleep time and every waking action we did. We had to be back in camp at a certain curfew time or face harsh punishment. Rules were stringent and enforced without question. The guards told us they shot prisoners for any suspicion of misconduct, although I did not understand this is what they said in the beginning of my imprisonment. Their loudly spoken harsh words terrified me as did their actions, especially the first time I actually did see a prisoner die in my presence for no reason that I could determine. At this blatant disrespect for life, I cringed in fear.

The routine I followed for work in the camp continued for many months. I went to the forced labor job I was assigned with Henry and kept my nose clean. I ate the bad food and slept on the hard cold beds and attempted to rest as much as possible. I talked to very few people and stayed friendly with the guards and did favors for them if I could. I would empty garbage containers or sweep floors for the uniformed men who ruled my world at night. Anything extra I could do to help them might keep me in their good graces and save my life.

Upon my arrival in Hamburg, I began to learn information about the city I had no reason to have known previously. This was a big and beautiful seaport city with many large historical buildings. Sometime after I got there, I found postcards in the church camp of important places in the city. I kept them hidden as proof I had been here. These unique documents gave priceless representations of important landmarks in Hamburg and how they looked before the war. After the destruction from the bombings in Hamburg was over, some of the buildings shown on the cards would never again be recognizable.

In 1940, Hamburg was the second largest city in Germany next to Berlin and contained an important waterway to aid in keeping the war effort going strong. The population was nearly two million and now included POWs taken from several locations across Europe. Men from various European countries were forced to live in concentration camps and work in labor camps in this city and across Germany. Able-bodied Jewish men from primarily Poland and Germany were also put to work here, however, they were treated much worse than the rest of the workers and eventually some were murdered, so I heard.

Hamburg was a relatively nice city when I first arrived in 1941. Rows upon rows of tall stately buildings lined the center of the city. Beautiful Gothic style churches occupied entire street blocks. Massive bridges crossed over the Elbe River and the landscape was riddled with trees barren of leaves from the fall season. All were left undisturbed prior to the bombings. At this point in the war, Hamburg remained a beautiful area soaking in the warmth of limbo.

Postcard picture of St Catherine's Church in Hamburg, prewar. It was heavily damaged during WWII in an air raid on July 30, 1943.

Postcard of City Hall Hamburg in 1939; The site of the Nazi surrender to the British Army in 1945 (untouched during WWII).

Postcard of Hamburg-Bergedorf, Germany, in 1936.

Most of the desirable city would never look the same after the bombs started coming on a daily basis. I called the bombs "those big babies." Everything they hit was destroyed. Many civilians were accidently killed by the Allies and became collateral damage in order to encourage the Nazis to surrender.

One of the worst bombings during WWII in Germany occurred in Hamburg on July 1943. At the time, I had no idea of the scope of damage left behind. I only knew I had miraculously survived one of many severe attacks I would personally witness. Nothing I had seen in my life so far compared to the horror of the destruction left by the bombs dropped on the mighty city of Hamburg during WWII.

After being in Germany for a couple days, I found out all POWs were treated like slaves. We were not privileged to have the same rights the German people had, although even the rights of these citizens had also been severely compromised by the Nazis. The Gestapo conspired to construct many laws and rules for their prisoners. The Poles, the Jews, and any of the other POWs were treated like enemies of the Germans. We could not go to restaurants and eat good food. Only the Germans could have the best food and shop for groceries. We ate what was served to us in the camps or starved. Meals were slim and normally not healthy. Thin soups were common as were bugs in the bread. Starvation of the prisoners was part of Hitler's plan to weaken us and prevent retaliation.

The Nazis had strict rules about women and curfews. POWs could not associate with any woman. If a prisoner got caught with a lady, he would most likely be shot. Marriage was forbidden. There was an eight o'clock curfew every night in Germany. If anyone being held in the camps got caught on the street after curfew, he risked being eliminated. The Gestapo thought nothing about shooting a POW without asking him why he was out past the required time to be in his assigned concentration camp. Rules were strictly enforced.

The German people walked by POWs on the streets and ignored us. They turned their heads away from us in disgust. They saw the cruel treatment of the Gestapo and SS toward the POWs. The local people knew we were starving. I guess they were relieved we were Hitler's prisoners and they were not. I couldn't understand how they were unable to sympathize with us and try to do something to help. The Nazis had control of everything—even the minds of the German people!

All the Polish prisoners had to wear a letter P on their coat sleeves in order to be easily identified by the Gestapo soldiers who were the official Nazi police force in Germany. The Russian prisoners were treated the same as the Poles and wore RUS on their coat sleeves. Jews were identified by the star on their coat sleeves and a tattooed number on their forearms, although I rarely saw them.

During their captivity, all POWs were required to carry identification (ID) provided to them by the Gestapo. The ID I carried on my body at all times consisted of a picture of me along with my signature printed on a glossy piece of photo paper taken at the time of my inspection in Berlin. The ghastly likeness of me was attached to a foldable piece of gray cloth. The heavy material of the document could be folded twice and allowed for numerous machine stamps dating my arrival at each concentration camp location I had been taken to. By the end of the war, I had several different stamps on the cloth due to having moved a few times when previous camps I had been in were destroyed.

Picture on my cloth Nazi POW ID.

Every POWs had to carry his ID card with him and not having an ID in his coat could mean a death sentence if an officer stopped him on the street and asked for it. Pleading usually did no good. No ID and he would shoot you!

There were thousands of POWs and we all had to be accounted for daily. Therefore, all prisoners were sprayed each morning with an identifiable scent before leaving for work. The smell was putrid and another way the Nazis humiliated us. Strangely enough, the scent was used for dogs to track us if we escaped. I learned the purpose of the stinky smell when I saw someone try to run away one day. When the POW went missing, soldiers released the dogs. The angry beasts easily caught the escaped prisoner and tore at his skin until the soldiers arrived to shoot him. Sometimes, the guards would stand by laughing and watch the dogs shred the person to pieces as a warning to the rest of us to obey their rules and not try to leave. The sight was pitiful to bear. By the grace of God, I was spared being used as an example of this cruel treatment and the possibility of suffering an excruciatingly painful death. To me, trying to escape seemed ridiculous.

POWs lived in fear of losing their lives from minute to minute. If anyone acted suspiciously, Nazi soldiers had the right to shoot any of them on sight for no particular reason. Hitler made his own rules and eventually authorizing murderous actions would constitute war crimes on the part of the Nazi Party once WWII ended.

I do say Hitler was a crazy, bad man, and sadly enough, many people did what he told them to do and followed his plan. There were some who didn't agree with his murderous ways, and before the war was over, Hitler's own German people tried to kill him three times I knew of. Some of his staff were among those who tried to turn against his idea for world dominance and they were executed. If they made a wrong move, he will kill them no matter who they were.

Killing people on a whim was a horrible thing Hitler allowed his soldiers to do in his name. When I heard the stories from other prisoners or witnessed murders, I felt like I was in a bad, bad nightmare dating back to the minute I was taken away from my parents by those Nazi soldiers who were obeying Hitler's commands and instituting his war psychology. I had a plan too. Mine was to survive.

CHAPTER ELEVEN

Working for Henry Jansen

I officially began working for the Nazis doing forced labor on October 18, 1941, in Hamburg-Altona, Germany, for Henry Jansen. He owned a coal business called Kohlenhandel and managed a large part of the coal supply being used by the Nazis to run war factories. He guarded the black gold without question for his own safety as Hitler ordered him to do. In my eyes, he followed orders from the Gestapo and did not make any waves in order to stay alive himself.

Henry's coal business made him an important person to Hitler. He helped to keep the war operational with his coal deliveries and facilitated the manufacturing of fuel for the factories. He was not at all like Hitler. Mr. Jansen was a kind man who did what he had to do to comply with Hitler's orders and survive the war as well as make a living for his family. In the beginning of my imprisonment, it was my fortune to be assigned to work for him.

Henry was a good boss. I had no problem with him. I went to work every morning and did the jobs he told me to do. I was kind of like Henry was to Hitler only Henry was not a prisoner. I was a good worker. We both came to trust and respect each other, and he became the kind of dad I never had. Imagine a Nazi supporter being like a father to me!

While I worked for Henry Jansen doing the coal business for the Nazis, he lived in a big house outside Hamburg near Altona, close to his main warehouse and business. He supplied the coal to Hitler, and in spite of his aiding the Nazi war effort, he was an honest and pleasant man.

Hitler's other military leaders like Hermann Goering, on the other hand, were terrible men. Hermann for one used his position to gain wealth and success through corruption and he became more evil with time. He ordered Jews be eliminated from the economy of Germany, which ultimately lead to the suggestion of their extinction from society beginning in 1938. He became richer every day by stealing confiscated wealth from the Jews during the war. He ordered Jews in Poland be sent to the Warsaw Ghetto and eventually to death camps as part of his plan in the Nazi organization to coordinate a final solution to the Jewish question and annihilate them.

Goering was able to accomplish these goals because Hitler placed him second in command over all of Germany's armed forces and in control of the total Nazi plan for supremacy. Goering's loyalty gave him a voice in encouraging Hitler to force men to work in his factories as well as deal with the problem of the Jews. He used seven hundred thousand men in forced labor to work for him during WWII. He was the creator of the secret police and founder of early concentration camps. At the onset of the war, Hitler named Goering to be his successor. They were two of a kind in my mind! I had hoped to never come across Mr. Goering in the war!

After I worked for Henry all day, I returned to the concentration camp and the barracks in the city of Hamburg, where I was ordered to sleep when I was not working. During the first few months of working all day, I was so tired some nights I could hardly walk back to the camp. At these times, the older POWs would get under my arms and help me walk. We were careful not to let the Gestapo see me being helped. If they thought I was too weak to work, they might shoot me! Some sick POWs had already been sent away, and I later discovered some had been sent to be killed at death camps along with the Jews.

When I became one of thousands of non-Jewish Polish men forced into hard labor during WWII, the first job I had to do at Henry's was to unload the coal from the gondolas. The coal came on these boats down the Elbe River on a daily basis after loads were taken off of tankers from the North Sea. Once the shipment arrived at the warehouse, I would carry the heavy bags on my neck up six flights of stairs and store the black gold in the top of storage buildings for future use.

On occasion, I rode with Henry delivering the coal to the warehouses. Henry knew he may be putting me at risk, so I did this only in an emergency to help him. Prisoners were not allowed to be given any special tasks requiring authority or giving them any sense of freedom. I did trust Henry with my life and did what he asked me to do.

As a prisoner of war, I was not paid for any of the work I did and was fed very little. The Gestapo treated me inhumanely as well as the other POWs. I was spat at, kicked, laughed at, and sometimes struck with a gun if I wasn't walking fast enough on the street in front of them. Keeping up my strength and spirits was tough.

I kept the POW ID cloth inside my coat at all times and never forgot to carry it with me. I could have been shot right there on the spot where I stood in front of an SS officer if he asked to see my ID and I had neglected to have it. This would have been the end of my life. I was on guard at all times for the sake of survival. For three and a half years, I lived as if I were being watched and constantly looked over my shoulder for potential danger!

When the Nazi soldiers brought me to Germany, I did not understand why. I got acquainted with the reason by listening to everything I could. I learned as war spread across Europe, the fuel supply for the war had declined. In order to keep the Germans in control, manpower had to be obtained for many operations. Men were needed to make ammunition, work on farms, and in coal factories. In 1942, Hitler ordered two hundred thousand men be brought to Germany from Eastern Poland and Ukraine for forced labor. All were necessary to support the war.

I traveled from the Nazi camp in the old church to work for Henry day after day. I worked very hard for him not only because it was expected of me but I respected Henry for his good treatment of me. The main job I did for him consisted of carrying a hundred pounds of coal to storage over and over for long hours every day. The coal had to be safely stored for future use in German factories. I did this job all day every day for months and months. Fortunately, I was quite strong from all the work I had done in Brzesciany before the war. I'm quite positive growing up and doing lots of chores and walking many miles to get food for our family definitely helped me to survive. Even though past work experiences toughened my body as a young man, nothing I had previously done really prepared me for the hard labor I now had to do. Survival was both a physical and mental challenge I had to face daily. I could have easily given up and let the Nazis shoot me. No way. I was made of strong Bednarz heritage, and I refused to give up my life for criminals as I saw them.

I turned eighteen years old about six weeks after being taken to Germany by force as a POW. At this young age, doing hard labor for the Nazis was difficult. Having accepted my fate, I tried to do the best I could. I used psychology on people to help me stay alive. I kept a nice look on my face when I met the Gestapo on the way to work. I said, "Yes, sir," in German to the soldiers in command as soon as I learned the words. I was careful not to make any bad decisions that might get me killed.

Life was different for the POWs in Germany than for the local people. Established German laws meant nothing for the POWs. By legal standards in Germany, a person had to be twenty-one years old to be employed. I was seventeen when I arrived! Age did not matter to the Nazis. Even though I did turn eighteen about six weeks after Nazi soldiers took me to Germany, I was far from the age of most German workers. It was war and no one cared about the forced labor workers. No matter. Things could always have been worse for me! I might have been forced to clean out the extermination ovens in the death camps like I had heard some of the prisoners were doing. According to POW's I heard talking in the concentration camps in the dead of night when sleep was impossible for me. I heard these whispered rumors and couldn't imagine having to work in such a place.

The German Secret Police (Gestapo) were set up by Hermann Goering to investigate any criminal activity aimed at the Nazi Party as well being in control of all people in forced labor. These evil men ruled the POWs with brute force and their presence at concentration camps was unmistakable. Anyone who did not follow the Nazi rules was beaten, shot, or put in solitary confinement by these Hitlerdominated officials and starved as an example to others. If you refuse to work, they make your life hell. I tried always to do what I was told. I followed the rules and made my situation as comfortable and safe as it could be. Oh, how I learned life wasn't fair at an early age!

Can you believe the German people did believe Hitler would make Germany a better place to live? Who was Hitler kidding? He was a murderer. He was a liar. He even tried to take away my religion and all the other religions. Hitler said the Lutheran and Catholic and all other churches had to disappear. He ordered religious symbols be destroyed. In the place of these symbols, he placed Swastikas. Hitler called the Swastika the immortal symbol of Germany. To me, the Swastika represented a symbol of death and destruction and certainly of prejudice.

I believe the German people became ashamed of their mistake in trusting Hitler as the rumors of mass killings circulated around their country. They were afraid of Hitler, of course! He took away their religious freedom and their holy leaders. Thousands of priests and ministers throughout Nazi Germany were persecuted, arrested, and sent to concentration camps. When Hitler spoke publicly, he told the German people he was far too important a person to be compared to Jesus. He allowed no one to speak about Jesus Christ. Talk of God angered Hitler. Secretly in my heart, the Almighty Father would always be my only hope for escape and salvation. Hitler could not take away the Lord who lived in my heart.

During the war, I found out there would be no church in the Hitler's Germany. There was no Christmas or Easter for he would not allow religious worship or celebrations of any kind. After arriving in Hamburg I realized talking about God might get me killed. All I had in this foreign land was the prayers I had learned as a child. For my own safety, I prayed in silence and no one ever heard the words I said to Jesus or Mary under by breath every day.

Nazi propaganda circulated endlessly during the war. Hitler's faithful military followers all wore the Swastika on the shoulder of their uniforms and proudly displayed the symbol from the windows of homes. This was Hitler's sign for world Nazi power. The disfigured angled crossed Ss meant nothing good to me. It merely symbolized murder, pain, and suffering. Never had I known such human hatred as was represented by this flag which bore the grotesque SS figure.

CHAPTER TWELVE

Life in the Camps

During the war, the labor I did continued to get more difficult. After hauling coal all day long, I was exhausted and hungry from lack of food and sleep. My fellow prisoners and I were always tired and longing for nourishment at the end of each day. None of us got much sleep or enough food in the camp at night. Our beds were made of straw on top of slabs of cement. Each of the beds was stacked three high and separated by wood posts. Our aching bones and the sounds of the night made our sleep difficult. The rats, the moans of the dying, and the drones of the bomber planes also influenced how well we all rested for the night. Our physical weakness increased day by day and prisoners died quite often.

Personally, I was cold at night. The room where I slept for many months was large and noisy. Explosions from the bombs came more often one after the other despite the darkness of the evening and expectations of a lull in the activity of the war at night. Badly needed rest from hard work never came easy for me with the lurking fear of death and the chill to my bones nearby. I never knew if I would survive to see the next day. When I wasn't too tired to sleep, I prayed for my life to be spared. As I lay in the straw bed at night questioning the path my life would take, the answers never came. I held on knowing one day I would understand the reason for existing on this earth, and I continually hoped to see my family again.

The food in the camps was terrible. Some days we were given only a small bowl of corn slop and a little piece of bread to eat.

Sometimes, I found maggots in the bread. The bugs in the food did not bother me. I picked anything unusual out of my food and ate it!

At night, I felt especially and incredibly hungry. Sometimes, I took the bread from the day's meal and saved it for later. On occasion, a piece of foul-smelling sausage was a rare treat. There were days the watery soup served to us had unidentifiable pieces of vegetable—obviously not the normal corn. I tried not to think about what it was I was eating. Staying strong became more difficult as time went on, even though I forced myself to eat all I could.

After the war, I never could get the taste and sight of the food I had eaten out of my mind. Because of the rotten food I was forced to eat in the camps, I have to say there have been foods I could not stomach again. One of them was creamed corn. This was one of our main staples every day in the camps. That kind of slop still made me sick years later if I tried to eat any after I was free and could eat whatever I wanted. Corn on the cob is the only similar vegetable I like nowadays. Getting a bad memory about food was no good. Sometimes, people in America did not understand my eating habits, and I was not able to tell them why I didn't want to eat it and make them believe as I did about the food.

The lack of decent food during the war caused me to lose strength in my body. There were days I was so tired and weak at the end of the day that I would stumble back to the camp. The other prisoners encouraged me to eat when I was too tired. We helped each other to stay strong. Mostly everyone was starving. It was said death rates were as high as 50 percent in some camps.

Conditions at the church camp were barely livable. People were dying from sickness and starvation. The Nazis didn't care. When someone died, the person disappeared and someone else was in their place the next day. Respect for human life was never a concern for the Nazis.

I was so lucky to be working for Henry, however, the concentration camp was not a pleasant place to return to after work. Henry never scolded me or made me feel bad. Some of the other prisoners talked of being threatened and beaten at their job sites. I had it better than most POWs.

After I had been in Germany a few months, I got acquainted with the language. Soon I could understand Henry when we talked. He was interested in me. For some reason, he took me on like a son and knowing how to communicate with him became a great help to me. The only good thing about having to be imprisoned during the war was having a man like Henry to care about my well-being.

One day, Henry asked me why I looked so sad.

"Jozef, what is the matter?" he prodded.

"I am hungry," I said. "I am coming to work to do hard labor for eleven hours a day, and I get almost no food to eat at the camp."

It may surprise you, I did complain to my boss. I was so hungry and I didn't care what I had to do to get some help. I did get mad at my situation sometimes, and I wasn't afraid Henry would hurt me. Other Nazi employers may have killed me. Not Mr. Jansen! I felt lucky to be able to tell him these things. As a genuinely fair and nice man, Henry could not have been a better boss.

When I told Mr. Henry Jansen how bad I felt about my life and how hungry I was, he told me he knew being a prisoner of war must have been terrible for me. On that day, he invited me to come to his house at lunchtime. He said his wife would fix me something to eat. I knew eating with a Nazi official or his family was strictly against the rules. Because I was so hungry, I agreed to go to his house. Let the Gestapo kill me, I thought to myself. Things were getting pretty tough for me by now, and I was just plain starving. During my working hours for Henry, I was required to eat at the POW food distribution centers which served the usual thin soup slop. I never felt satisfied with the skimpy meals they served.

I was not the only hungry POW! All the POWs were underfed. Some prisoners were almost skeletal in appearance. The Nazi psychology of potential starvation instilled fear in all prisoners so they would keep working. Some of them were so weak, they died trying to work. What purpose did death serve the Nazis when workers were lost? I did not understand. But again, what purpose did any of this war serve? Henry offered to give me food in secret, and as a result of eating his food, I did not starve to death due to his generosity and sacrifice. For that, I would be forever grateful to him.

On the first day Henry invited me to come to his home and sit at the table with the family and eat, I went without thinking twice. Mrs. Jansen could see I was skin and bones. She fed me wonderful food, and from then on, she always brought me something to eat during the day. She would bring food to the workers' shack even though doing so was against the Nazi regulations. The Jansens didn't care about the rules. Mr. Jansen was a high-ranking official, and I figured he was safe from the Gestapo. So I ate his food and the meals were delicious.

You know I am quite sure the Jansens probably saved my life with their kindness to me. I have never forgotten their generosity. I survived the war partly because of them and planned to express my gratitude as long as they were alive. My favorite story about Mrs. Jansen's cooking is a funny one. On the particular day I speak about, she invited me for supper at their house after work. Usually, I didn't go there so late because of the Nazi curfew. In this case, I figured I had plenty of time to eat and get back to the camp by 8:00 p.m. curfew. After all, she said she had made something special for me, and I didn't want to disappoint either one of us.

When I came to eat supper with the family that evening, Mrs. Jansen served up something I had to refuse. She walked into the room where we ate with a plate of food heaped with white and shiny, tubular, slimy, pieces of meat. When she offered me the tray, I told her, "I don't eat worms!" She just laughed and offered me something else to eat.

The next day, I came from the workers shack for lunch, and Mrs. Jansen said had made sandwiches for me, which I ate very fast since I was hungry.

She asked me, "How was the sandwich?"

I said, "It was delicious," as I bit into another.

"I ground up those worms you wouldn't eat last night," she said with a strong German accent and a mischievous grin on her face.

I nearly spit the food out of my mouth. I laughed so hard. Then she told me those worms were shrimp. I didn't know. I had never seen shrimp or eaten it before.

Mrs. Jansen had gotten me good with her trick on me! We all had a fun time over my mistake. She had made me laugh, and laughter was a rare occurrence for nearly everyone during the war. I felt wonderful to be so happy and gaining strength with such wonderful people helping me out.

While at Henry's place, I worked with a polite young Polish man named Bronek. Our boss could see we had become friends, and he surprised us by buying us each a nice suit and taking a picture of us we could carry inside the jackets we wore. I carried this picture in my coat everywhere I went to remind me of my friend.

Picture of my friend, Bronek, on the left and me on the right taken in Hamburg-Altona 1942 during the war.

Bronek was a good Polish man who was in captivity with me. We shared similar physical appearance of black hair and brown eyes. At times, I saw the look of fear in his eyes of uncertainty about what would become of us both here in the frightful land of Hitler. Eventually, we were separated in the war, and I never saw him again. His picture gave comfort to me later on during bad times in my life as a POW when I thought about our friendship together. Henry took our photo somewhere in Hamburg, Germany, in 1942 and I felt grateful to him for this favor.

During my time as a POW doing hard labor during WWII in Germany, I was required to work every day of the week including Saturday and Sunday. If the gondola came on the railroad with twenty-five tons of coal on Christmas, I had to work. Nazis did not care about holidays anyway. Rain or shine, snow and blizzard, there was work. The only excuse for anyone not going to work was death.

I kept working hard and tried not to think about the fate I had been forced to endure or my family back in Poland. Working as I did for Henry was such a lucky thing! To have a good boss like Mr. Jansen helped me forget the bad nights in the camps. I saw indignant and abusive treatment of other POWs happening around me all the time. My life in Germany could have been so much worse. Other prisoners were often beaten and whipped by their bosses or even killed.

I never missed work! In Nazi Germany, punishment for not going to work in the forced labor camps could be a twenty-five-day sentence at a death camp where Jews were exterminated. The worst known punishment given to the workers in the camps was making them clean the extermination ovens or bury the dead in mass graves if available. Some workers who were being punished never returned from where they were sent.

The Gestapo did many bad things in my eyes. Prisoners who did not follow the rules were used as examples for the other prisoners. One day, I witnessed someone in my camp refused to go to work due to illness. The Gestapo beat him senseless. The beatings left disgusting open sores on his body. I witnessed other men in the camps with unhealed, draining wounds. Such sores as those I saw emitted an unbearable stench like a dead animal on the road. The smell would pierce the gentle nostrils of my nose and threaten to make me vomit. After seeing the cruel treatment of sick prisoners by the Nazi authorities, I never missed work no matter how bad I felt.

Life in the camps was pathetic for all the POWs. Never could I have imagined such a pitiful sight in my eyes as these camps. The Nazis who caused these things were devils to us all. Human beings did not deserve to be abused and purposely mistreated like those of us in the concentration facilities. Occasionally Jewish prisoners would be brought to the camp and made to wear pajamas all day long and others were made to walk around the camps naked to see if they were sick. Quickly, some disappeared as fast as they had come. I didn't know at the time where the SS had taken them. Today, I realize they had been sent to be murdered.

CENTER PHOTOGRAPHS

Mom and Dad Bednarz, Matteas (on left) and Stanley (on right) in Poland early 1950s.

Jozef Bednarz, 1951.

Jozef Bednarz in the middle in postwar Germany with other Polish soldiers.

Jozef in formal military Polish Army uniform in postwar Germany.

Visiting my mother's grave in Klodzko, Poland, in 1995.

Visiting the Polish-American WWII cemetery in Luxemburg in 1997.

Visiting General George Patton's Grave in Luxemburg in 1997.

The Bednarz Family with ten children present at Katherine and Bruce Ritchie's wedding in 2007: (front row) Leanne, Sandye, Sharon and Jozef, (back row) Mary, Barb, John, Jan, Katherine, Bruce, Peggy, Tom, Rob. (Missing: Angie and Theresa.)>

Angie Curell daughter of Jozef

Theresa Gerdis-daughter of Jozef

CHAPTER THIRTEEN

Bombing Hamburg

Hamburg was a beautiful city before the Allies came with their bombs and started the siege on the Nazis in January of 1943. I did not blame the Allies for the destruction they caused. They were in Germany to stop the spread of the Nazi takeover in Europe and end the war. Death and destruction of property was inevitable, however, the constant blast of exploding gunpowder frightened me and put my life in danger.

When I came to Hamburg as a prisoner, there were big beautiful trees along the roadside where I walked to catch the sidecar to go to my forced labor job at Henry's place. Once the frequent bombings by the Allies began, the scenery changed drastically. Charred branches draped the once colorful greenery lining the cobblestone streets. I saw bricks lying everywhere blown out of their original rightful places in the perfect silhouette of sturdy buildings. A chalky dust from massive explosions of cement structures covered the paths leading to remaining homes and businesses. Destruction became more widespread and noticeable in the city day by day.

One day as I was walking along the white powdery dirt-covered path to work, I could hear the birds singing. The day was unusually sunny and peaceful. Not for long! As soon as the majestic musical sounds ceased, I sensed something was wrong. Suddenly, there was a deafening explosion and the war changed the vision I had of a hopeful life in an instant.

When the loud boom shook the earth, there were many people together on the same path as me walking on the street to go to work.

For the first time in my life, I would witness one of many bombs fall to the earth from the sky directly in front of me. The exploding shrapnel hit the ground with such intense force I was knocked to my knees and blinded by black smoke. A fireball the size of a city block blazed uncomfortably close to my face.

When those "big babies" fell out of the sky and I was thrown off my feet and fell to the ground, I picked myself up and dusted off the dirt from my thinning trousers. I glanced around the area not sure what to do next. I could see the melting asphalt of the street swallow up people and burn them alive. Large gaping holes in the ground several hundred feet in front of me held remnants of massive missiles and probably human beings. Numerous people who had been walking on the street a second ago had now disappeared from my eyes. Body parts were mixed with the dirt and human skin hung from the tree branches above. Horrible. It was horrible.

Devastation was everywhere, and miraculously, I had survived. I hurried on to Henry's place with tears streaming down my face.

Days later, I would hear news of the historic massive bombing attack by the United States and British Allies across Hamburg, some of which I had witnessed for two days in July of 1943.

After the bombing, I continued to walk on down the blood-stained street to my work site as if nothing had happened. The hot summer air brushed my cheeks and the burn of gun powder stung my nostrils as I cried for those who died. For my own safety, I could not stop to help the injured. And there was nothing I could do to help the dead but pray for their souls.

Similar bombings continued on a much smaller scale on a daily basis for a few days, and then there was quiet while the planes apparently moved on to another location.

I remember there were other airplane attacks during the years I was in Hamburg. Sometimes in the winter, out of nowhere, the snow would start to fall after a bomb had fallen. I could see the pure white flakes flutter to the ground and turn red as they melted in the blood of the fallen victims of another air raid. I often walked in an area where moments before humans had lived and breathed the same air as I had. Their flesh hung from the trees above as I cried silently in pain. War was a bad, bad thing! I wondered how I would ever be able to forget the horror of the things I had seen during this war if I did manage to survive.

On the day of the historical Hamburg bombing, blood dripped at my feet from the branches above me as I quietly sauntered down the road block knowing there was not a thing I could have done to save any of the people in the path of the bombs. In the lightning flash of a second, many people were dead. My heart cried for their loved ones, and I felt selfishly fortunate to be alive.

The first time a bomb went off near me, I went into emotional shock. The sight of human flesh hanging from the trees above my head haunted me for days and still does today. I had to remind myself how lucky I was every day I lived through the war. I was blessed. For three and a half years, I worked for the Germans and risked my life nearly every day. After the first bombs came, they continued to drop from the sky planes for over the next two years. Hamburg changed into a junkyard right before my eyes and life became more unbelievable for me as each day passed. I wondered if I would survive the war and just when this nightmare would end for me and the world.

Seeing the bombs hit and kill other human beings was traumatic. Witnessing the cleanup of their bodies after the explosion was even worse. The remains of the dead including their body parts had to be picked up off the street. There was a lot of terrible work to be done, and I saw the Nazi police forcing people to pick up bones and pieces of flesh lying around on the ground and put them in baskets. The streets had to be disinfected because of the blood everywhere. What an unbelievable sight to try to put out of my mind.

I had lived at the church camp for about a year when my routine was disrupted by the natural progression of the war. I came to know most of the other eighty POWs who stayed with me during that time. I had made friends in spite of the war and of being under constant surveillance by the Gestapo. The POWs from the church had helped me get through the most terrifying year of my life. Many were my friends and I had not considered how my situation might change.

These POW friends of mine at the church camp taught me how to protect myself the best I could from the bombs. When I first arrived in Hamburg, the air was pretty quiet. As the war progressed, the bombs started to come more frequently. Other POWs helped me become familiar with the sound of the planes coming right before a bomb exploded.

On one particular day, I had a weird feeling as I prepared to leave for work in the morning. Something told me to get out of the church camp immediately. So I left quickly not knowing why. When the hair on my neck made me cold, I started to almost run out of the building. Then it happened.

I was about a block away from the home I had known for the last year when I heard the drone of a fighter plane and the crash of a bomb moments before the church camp exploded. A missile had landed right on the top of the building. All I could see was a huge cloud of smoke, fire, and dust. The old church building and everyone still inside had died from the bomb blast.

Realizing I had lost most of my friends in the church camp, I crumbled to the muddy earth in despair. I hated Hitler with all my being at that moment. The deaths of those men who had become like family to me were his fault. Life seemed unfair in so many ways.

Slowly, I turned around to see the whole block had disappeared. There was nothing left. The entire structure of the church had been leveled. Most of the POWs were still inside getting ready to go to their jobs. Now they were all dead. I was devastated. This was war. I could not comprehend the hatred of the men in command here in Germany.

I arrived at work and informed Henry about the destruction of the church camp. He reported my survival of the bombing to the Nazi officials. We both knew I would need another place to sleep. The church camp had been an adequate shelter for me the last several months, and now I would have to be placed somewhere possibly less desirable. Such was my fate as a Polish POW of WWII.

By the end of the workday, I was assigned to a new concentration camp to sleep in at night. Unfortunately, my new sleeping quarters were much farther away from Henry's place, and I had to ride the train to work in the mornings. Skepticism threatened my security about the new arrangements I now faced.

When the Gestapo moved the few surviving POWs of the church camp to different living quarters in northern Hamburg, I had to walk to an underground train station in the morning to get to work. Although Altona was now located much farther to the south of the city from where I resided at night, Henry refused to let me go from his service. Therefore, I would have to adjust to a new experience in traveling differently to work.

On the first morning I had to take the train to work, the steam-powered locomotive moved rather fast and made me dizzy. I thought I would vomit. Fearing I might be mistaken for a sickly prisoner by the Nazi guards on the train and be hauled away, I hung on tightly to the rail on the inside of the car and took deep breaths. I eventually got used to this new mode of transportation that lasted forty-five minutes to my job destination and landed safely in Altona.

I disliked the new concentration camp where I lived at night and the unpleasant ride to the assigned job site every morning. The sleeping quarters were crowded in the old brick building where I now slept at night. The beds were again made of straw on cement and I was colder at night than ever. Many of the POWs were sickly and weak. I was afraid I might also become ill so I prayed hard to stay well.

I did not have to stay at this new camp for more than a couple months because it too was bombed out, and once again I was moved to another foreign part of Hamburg. The third camp I was taken to was rundown barracks. Cockroaches were everywhere. They crawled all over me and the other prisoners at night. I shiver to think of this. I don't know why the Gestapo couldn't kill those bugs. They did not care about any of us! Hitler made them that way.

A few months later, the third camp I was in got bombed out too while I was away at work. I told Henry when I went to do my job for him the next day because I had nowhere else to go. He said I could stay with him. He would make sure the authorities knew.

Henry had a huge home with plenty of places for me to sleep at night. I preferred to rest out in the workers shop at night while

Henry went to the bunker with his family after dark, although he wanted me to sleep in the same bunker below his house. I reassured him I would come and join him and the others later on. I did not, figuring if the bombs came, I would be buried alive. I believed if the house above a bomb shelter took a direct hit, the people in the bunker could be crushed or suffocated. I wanted to be near the outdoors where I felt safer, and Henry didn't have to know where I stayed for now.

At night, I would sneak out of the worker's shed or out of the basement of Henry's house and listen to the London Public Radio. I listened to the London radio station in the English language. I would hear the announcers talking on the radio about when they thought the bombs would be coming. I enjoyed listening to the radio, and I learned some of the English language a little at a time.

The news from the radio gave me new hope. The British were optimistic the Allies would defeat Hitler. This was the best feeling for me. I would hear reports the Allies were closing in on Berlin. I prayed my freedom was coming soon. War tired me so utterly and completely.

I stayed at Henry's house for many months. This was my best time during the war. Henry was like a dad to me and much nicer to me than my own dad had been even though he had to be a Nazi supporter. I gave thanks to my God for His blessings to me with Henry. I was in heaven for sure living with Henry compared to the hell I had experienced previously sleeping in the bug-filled cold barracks in the Hamburg concentration camps.

Henry's house had not been bombed when I stayed with him. He and his family slept in the basement at night, which served as a bunker. Henry was afraid the bombs might kill him and his family during the night. This is why they chose to sleep in the bunker. He was very careful to protect those he loved.

One night, Henry caught me outside of the bunker. He was mad as hell at me when he found out I did not stay with the rest of his family. He was fond of me, and I was treated like his own son after a few months. I supposed he was afraid I would die if he didn't protect me, and this caused his anger at my disobedience. We had become very close, and I hated to disappoint him, so I stayed close to the bunker from then on.

Due to the constant bombings occurring during the war, Henry's coal for the government had to be kept in attic storage. For this reason, the job I did for him was to carry the coal on my neck up six flights of stairs every day for safe keeping until its use. The coal had normally been kept in cellars or bunkers before the war. After the chaos started, basements became bunkers and served as bomb shelters, leaving no room for anything else. Even so, people may have been just as unsafe in a bunker as the coal was up in the air once a bomb blew away a building over top of the people below. Contemplating such an incident to happen encouraged me to dislike any basement hideout.

The evil effects of war touched everyone, even Henry. After delivering coal to storage one evening late in the fall of 1943, I walked from Henry's business property to his place for supper and saw Henry's big home had been bombed. The worker's shack and the house were indistinguishable due to the destruction all around the area. I feared Henry, his wife, and their children—a son and daughter about my age—were all dead. Sadness filled my soul for these people who had been so good to me.

I didn't know what to do now that Henry had apparently died and went away from this earth. The loss of a man whose kindness and protection from so much bad left a deep sense of loss in my heart! I turned around in agony over Henry and his family's fate not knowing what to do from here on. I would be solely in the hands of the evil Nazis without Henry to watch over me.

I didn't know where to go after I saw the demolition caused by the bombs in Altona and at Henry's place. Hunger and shock gripped my being. With another POW accompanying me to the horrific sight, and both confused as to our options, we started walking back to Hamburg together.

Hamburg and Altona were connected by city boundaries within a couple kilometers of each other. As we walked back to the larger city, we had much time to clear our heads and ponder the situation we were in. We made the lonely trip back to the warzone and my optimism waned as scattered thoughts filled my head about all I been through since I arrived in Germany after being taken forcefully by the Nazis. I wondered what would happen next.

In my mind's eyes, I saw Henry's house bombed out, and sickness to myself threatened to overwhelm me. I felt a little better with someone to accompany me as I walked back to the main part of Hamburg, and we joined other Polish POWs gathering on the street going back to their own camps. Together, the POW who accompanied me and I knew of nothing of what we could do for shelter or food, so we walked around the city and tried to scavenge something to eat. We cared not if we got caught at this point, being extremely tired, hungry, and numb as we were.

After walking for what seemed like hours, my newest POW friend and I were so starved we decided to look in the garbage for food. The leftovers we found in the trash were quickly devoured.

After sleeping in an alley and waiting for morning to come, our day began with the hope of a sun-filled sky. However, I believed Henry was dead and sorrow threatened to destroy my joy. The warmth of the brilliant lighted sky gave me a reason to go on rather than to just lie in the street and die.

On this next morning, I arose from my resting place and slipped into a city soup line in an innocent attempt to ease painful hunger pangs. Making this choice ultimately became a bad mistake. What else was there for me to do? But I should not have forgotten I was a POW! The local soup lines were not for prisoners. The food in large pots being given away on the streets was for the hungry German people and not for the underprivileged forced labor workers.

Anticipating a nourishing breakfast, I waited patiently in the soup line. Then someone yelled at me and caught the attention of the Gestapo. Apparently my tattered POW jacket drew the attention of the local people in the crowd. Now I was in great trouble.

"Hey, what are you doing here?" an angry voice called out from the line behind me.

After my presence became a source of attention for everyone within hearing distance of the unhappy person taunting me in the soup line, a nearby German soldier turned to look in my direction and investigate the disturbance. I was busted.

The Nazi authority had food distribution centers set up all over Hamburg for the poor German families. These hungry people were not about to share their food with me or any other POW! Most locals had done nothing to help alleviate the suffering of us innocent human beings from other countries who had been put in forced labor camps or others tortured or murdered in their country. Come on! I just wanted a bite to eat.

Before I could go any further in line and get something to eat, the Gestapo soldier came by and smelled me out. He grabbed the collar of my jacket roughly and pulled me out of the soup line and pushed me out into the street. Instantly, I became the obstacle of everyone's attention. Normally, I would not have made an attempt to break any rules or cause notice to myself, but at this point, I didn't care so much and I really needed to. Quickly, I decided if I were to survive the fate I had been handed so unfairly, I would need to change the attitude that could precipitate my death. I did not resist the officer's actions toward me and merely apologized for my mistake.

"I am sorry, sir. I did not realize I cannot be here." I pleaded ignorance in broken German.

The Gestapo soldier did not allow me to have any food of course. He had identified me as a Polish prisoner by the P on my coat and left me to wait for him while he went off in search of other violators of the law.

After an inspection of the soup line by the Nazi police, other prisoners were also caught trying to get food and were all taken away with me at gunpoint. No exceptions were ever made for the falsely imprisoned foreign people forced to do labor in the war who were breaking the rules. We were bums to the local people and hunger was no excuse to be in their public soup line.

"Stop!" the soldiers belted out in sharp German tongue. We stood still and waited to see what would happen next. Any sudden movement could be the end of our lives. Most Gestapo soldiers had no problem shooting POWs without a specific reason. In this case, we had broken their law and they had every right to kill us.

Since POWs were not allowed to congregate with the city folk to get free food, we had broken the law. More Gestapo soldiers joined in to round up the marked prisoners from the soup line. They pointed their guns at us and we were lucky they didn't shoot. We all must have had angels protecting us from harm! This, day the Nazi Gestapo had me and my POW partners at their mercy and they spared our lives. What a blessing!

The Gestapo shoved me and the rest of the POWs into the back of a rusty old military truck and took us to a camp I was unfamiliar with. Today, we would live knowing we were fortunate to have had our lives spared. A new camp meant we had been analyzed and determined to be useful in the Nazi work force.

We were not given any food at the camp when we arrived late at our newest home in the afternoon. Apparently, mealtime in the new residence had passed us by. I was starving and miserable. In that moment, I didn't really care if I lived or died.

I knew I was at the lowest point of my life on that day. I prayed for a change in the mental outlook I now portrayed to those who looked into my eyes. I had to hold on to thoughts of my family to keep me going.

Suddenly as if touched by some spiritual being for encouragement, I thought about my mom and my family and felt hopeful. I realized I had to be brave or I would certainly die and they would never see me again! I knew prayers for courage were in order. I seemed to have become a mere silhouette of a tortured man struggling to hang on to anything to motivate him to save himself.

CHAPTER FOURTEEN

Camp Helmstedt-Browsavery

When my ordeal in the street of the city came to an end, the Gestapo had moved me to a different concentration camp in a part of Hamburg I was unfamiliar with. The POWs I arrived with stayed together at the new prisoner facility for only one day. We were fed the usual slop and allowed to rest a little while the Nazi soldiers decided what to do with us. I always had a little fear about what my fate would be. Waiting never seemed to be a good thing for any prisoner. POWs tended to disappear much too easily.

Life in the concentration camps had changed frequently for me during the war. I failed to accurately anticipate what would happen next from month to month as the war drudged on endlessly. At times, I thought I might be set free. Other times, I feared I would be killed. Instead, the Nazis never failed to put me to work. I tried to use my psychology on the superiors in the camps every day to make myself useful to them and guarantee my survival. Each time I changed sleeping quarters I had to sniff out the right way to act.

On the evening of the first day in the new camp, I found myself being moved again when a German Army vehicle came and picked me up along with several other POWs. We were shipped to Camp Helmstedt near Browsavery. I was about to begin another new experience I wouldn't have chosen for myself.

I heard Hèrmann Goering's name mentioned during the transport. I knew anything associated with him meant nothing good for me. Goering was Hitler's primary supporter, a war party leader, and a major contributor to the war effort. I found out he controlled the bullet factory where I would now work. Goering would no doubt be a ruthless slave driver here with his orders strictly enforced by those in charge of operations.

The Nazi officials put us to work in one of many ammunition factories operated under Hermann Goering's authority. These facilities manufactured the artillery for the war that helped fuel his plan filled with a strategy for a Nazi worldwide takeover. He was an evil man without a conscious much like Hitler. Working under him was one place I did not want to be.

The job I performed at the ammunition factory proved to be the worst kind of work I had done in my life. The labor on the assembly line was difficult and the supervisors were mean and strict. They told us we had to make the artillery shells correctly, or we would be punished severely. We made very large bullets on an old and poorly maintained machine twenty-four hours a day. Errors were inevitable, and I was filled with fear of making mistakes.

The machines at the ammunitions factory were poorly balanced and wearing out. Making a functional bullet was difficult for anyone to do. I was afraid of what they would do to me if I made bad bullets. The Gestapo supervisors were always looking over my shoulder to make sure I worked hard and did the pattern correctly. I was. I made certain the work I did met the accuracy standards demanded by those in charge since my life depended on completing useable ammunition.

The bullets came off the assembly line oiled and slippery. The pieces we produced were hard to handle and heavy. I constantly feared I would produce a product failure which kept my nerves on edge all the time.

At night, I traveled along with the forced labor workers back to the prison camp. The concentration camp where we stayed was another primitive barracks. Our sleeping quarters were horrible at night. There were about five hundred prisoners crammed together in the same huge building. The air smelled of urine and feces. Mice and rats scampered around nibbling at our feet during the night. As usual, we slept on straw beds piled three high on top of hard cold cement as usual. The room temperature was freezing during the winter and sweltering hot in the summer and noisy like other camp quarters had been. I could hear the bombs coming at night more and more often than they had in the past. I never knew if I would live to see the next day or die from hunger, freeze to death, or be blown up by a bomb. I prayed for safety and to see my family again. I prayed a lot.

The POWs in this labor camp were starving here as well as in the others I had been in. We all worked twelve hours a day for little food. At night, some of us we more brave men would sneak out of the barracks. With so many prisoners to keep track of, the guards never missed the few of us who slipped out in the late evening in search of food. We went to the edge of the camp and into a nearby farmer's field to dig up potatoes with whatever tools we could find to break through the soil. We would steal the white vegetables from the ground and eat them raw since we were so hungry. This helped us not to starve and to have the energy to work at the factory. We were careful not to get caught. Like everywhere else, you get caught, they shoot you!

Eating rotten potatoes would be bad for anyone making such a mistake. Sometimes, the potatoes were contaminated with bacteria and made people so sick they died. I was one of the prisoners lucky enough to not get infected with bad germs from the fruits of the fields.

I think the potato food helped to save my life much as Henry's meals did. Many POWs died in the camps from lack of nutrition. The portions of bread we were given were very small and not enough to sustain a man doing hard labor. There just wasn't enough food for us hardworking men. Many of the men were skin and bones. I never saw men as skinny as I did during the war. I was fortunate to get some extra food and even luckier to have stayed healthy when I was with Henry. I thought about him a lot since the bombing at his residence. I hoped and prayed he and his family had survived the blast to their home.

Surviving the war was everyone's goal. Unfortunately for the Jewish people, they had it the hardest. The Gestapo did many mean things to the Jews during the war. One day, I saw a bomb hanging from a tree with the detonator still intact. I could see the live fuse coming off it. The explosive device probably weighed close to 850 pounds. I'm sure the Germans were afraid it would blow up if they tried to move it. So they went and got a few Jewish men to deactivate the dangerous remnant of war.

The imprisoned men who came to take the bomb apart were specialized in explosive ordinance disposal (EOD) I suppose. They carefully took the fuse apart. The Germans made them take the powder out of the bomb and completely disassemble it. The steel from the bomb would be melted down in the bullet factory and used again since the metal was of real good quality. The reason Jewish men were used to take the bomb apart was in case it exploded, they would die instead of the German officers. They always made the Jews do risky things and be in danger rather than risking their own lives.

In general, life was difficult for anyone imprisoned during the war. Stress levels were high and fear made everyone nervous. My own fear and nerves and hopeless feelings nearly got me killed more than once!

CHAPTER FIFTEEN

My Special Friend

While working under Nazi forced labor in the ammunition factory, I kept to myself and concentrated on my job until one day I saw a woman out of the corner of mine eyes who took my breath away. I had never seen such a beautiful lady as her in my life. She was an angel before these hungry tired eyes. A rare smile formed on the parched lips of this lonely Polish bachelor's face.

I learned the pretty lady at the factory was a paid local worker of German descent. She walked with grace and stunned my vision with a nice body and soft blue eyes while passing by my work area with ease. I had noticed her eyes glancing toward me several times since I started my job in this dreary, cold aluminum building. Now the aroma of her sweet feminine scent filled the air in which I breathed.

As I saw the events happening, a mutual attraction seemed to be occurring between me and the mysterious lady at the factory. The first time I got up the courage to wish her a good day, I spoke to her carefully and discreetly in broken German. Once we had greeted each other, we instantly became friends and she a special person in my daily camp life. We assumed a friendship from the minute we met.

Before our chance meeting in the factory, many other German women had given me the flirtatious eye and tempted my male attentions in the past here in this godforsaken war-torn country. This lady was different. She befriended me, and I was showered with kindness and sweetness by her. In order to protect me from prosecution by the

Gestapo, she used discreetness in initiating her conversations with me for my safety and hers.

With coal black hair and alluring brown eyes, I was a handsome young man who appealed to the ladies. At different times, I found German women following me around trying to get with me. I had to be careful. Relationships of any kind with local females were strictly forbidden according to the Nazi rules for the POW. The consequences of getting caught with a woman were brutal punishments and could prove fatal. A brief erotic encounter definitely would not be worth a little bit of fun if one had to die for the experience.

So what do you expect for a cute, young Polish bachelor? I was eighteen, nineteen, twenty, and twenty-one years of age as a POW during WWII. The ladies loved me! Unfortunately, I had to forget about my attractiveness in order to stay alive. Life was hard as a prisoner. I looked for ways to keep me sane and not being able to befriend women was not always an easy thing for a healthy young man to do. Constantly, I had to keep myself in check for my life depended on being smart.

The new lady friend I got acquainted with was different from other women who came around me on the streets in Hamburg. I wanted her to follow me around. She really didn't do that to me though. We just talked to each other at the factory at first and I found I liked her a lot. We had to be cautious when we spoke together at the factory because the Gestapo thought everyone had a conspiracy against them, especially people who whispered with one another. We exchanged understanding glances more than we conversed while doing our jobs at work in order to keep a low profile and avoid the suspicion of our Nazi supervisors.

Emma was her name. After a couple weeks, Emma and I started to have secret meetings when we completed our work for the day in the factory. We would walk along the dark alleys of Hamburg so no one would see us together. I was so happy to be with her and also scared for her. I did not want her to get hurt. She was a beautiful German lady who wasn't supposed to conspire with POWs. I feared the Gestapo for they were known to have tortured women in the past when their rules were disobeyed. The local people were well aware

German women had been raped or forced into marriages by the Nazi soldiers in spite of their good behavior. No woman could truly be safe.

After I met Emma, I continued my hard work in the factory every day in a much better state of mind. I felt a lot better knowing she would be waiting to see me after work. This woman was the best thing that happened to me during the war and really up to this point in my life. I loved her very much. Her kindness and beauty warmed my heart. Emma was the first lady I felt I had ever truly loved other than my sisters and my mom, whom I loved in an entirely different way.

Emma lived in Hamburg. She would sneak me breads and cakes she had baked herself at her home. Her treats helped me grow stronger than I had been in a long time, and therefore, my work got a little easier. She made my life happy and healthy. She taught me more German words than I already knew, helping me to better understand what I heard the Gestapo and other Nazi supporters discussing. I began to feel more confident in surviving the imprisonment forced upon me by Hitler and his appointed officials.

Much of Emma's life and history were a mystery to me. I didn't care. It was probably better for her if I did not know much about her. I trusted her. I loved her. That was enough for now. I started to think about being with her after the war. Now I had another dream to motivate me to live through the worst days of my life.

For a few months after our workdays were done, Emma and I met together especially when we could sneak away to a secluded area. We got emotionally closer to each other as time went on. Eventually, we talked about getting married after the war. I knew I wanted to be with her, and she expressed the same desire. I couldn't believe my fortune. She was the love of my life. In order for our situation to be perfect, I needed to be free. Then my mother could eventually meet her someday.

Emma and I had our secret places where we met in the evenings. We had to be very careful to be off the street by curfew. One evening, I hurried back to the POW camp later than usual after the two of us had lost track of time. Emma was not in as much danger as me when she broke off and headed to her home. On the other hand, I obviously had put my life in danger by being on the street after curfew.

I knew the deadline for being in camp had passed me by as I slithered through the blackness of the narrow winding path between decrepit brick buildings of downtown Hamburg. My heart pounded in my throat as I hurried toward the bunker I called home for the night. I prayed to arrive safely unnoticed by the security police I knew were around every corner.

Suddenly, a Gestapo officer stepped out of the darkness and blocked my progress as I hurried down the road. Fear gripped me. I knew this could be very bad as I felt my heart beating wildly in my ears. I prayed for the life I had treasured so carefully to be spared.

When the Secret State police officer halted me on the street, I smiled at him.

"What are you doing on the street?" he screamed at me in his sharp German tongue.

"I am running an errand for my boss at the factory, sir," I told him politely in a bad attempt to speak his native language.

He nodded back at me. Whew!

He said, "Hurry on, young man. Curfew time is going!"

"Yes. Thank you, sir," I addressed him kindly and saluted reverently.

I was so relieved. Can you believe my luck? I might have been shot for being on the street at that hour. I believe my fortune to be God given once more.

Emma and I continued to meet together on a regular basis. We were more careful to watch the time and listen to the curfew alarms after that fear-filled night I was nearly captured by the Gestapo.

When we met, she would hold my face in her soft hands and kiss me gently on the lips.

"Jozef, you are such a beautiful man! I love you so much," she told me one sunny, warm summer day behind the factory, far beyond the vision of my captors.

"My sweet heart, Emma, I love you too," I proclaimed to her in broken German with an aching heart.

"You have made me a happy woman," she spoke softly in perfect German as I struggled to understand her words.

"Perhaps you will never leave me, my love," I begged her with tears threatening to ruin my bravery.

"Never," Emma smiled tensely. We both feared what the future had in store for us both.

Our secret rendezvous continued on a regular basis until one Sunday evening when we agreed to get together after our workday had been cut unusually short. Somehow I sensed things were peculiar. An inborn perception of misfortune warned me when I was about to be adversely affected in the future I would soon face.

I arrived at the precise area where we had previously decided to meet and felt uncomfortably apprehensive. Emma had not arrived here yet. Immediately, I feared something bad had happened to her. She was always on time and had never previously not shown up when she promised she would.

I waited for a couple hours until curfew time came. I retired to the barracks with a sad heart crying for my dear Emma. At this time, I knew my life would not include Emma again.

The next day at work, Emma's absence from the ammunition factory became blatantly apparent when I arrived. I did not see her there ever again. Devastation consumed me. I tried to forget my special friend and let work take her off my mind.

On that first day after Emma missed our meeting, a crushing pain filled my chest and a feeling of a heavy weight pressed upon my burdened breastbone. My body was bearing the loss of her love, and later in the bunker that night, tears came to my eyes where I lay unable to sleep thinking of how I missed her tremendously. I knew something had gone wrong in her life, and there was possibly no way for me to ever know what had happened to her unless I saw her once more. I had to face the fact I might never know where she had gone.

Work in the bullet factory continued on at a boring pace until a few months later when I saw Emma. As I walked down the street to my bunker, I recognized the sweet lady I had come to love was walking across the road from me. At that moment, I knew my dreams of ever having her as my wife were over. She belonged to someone else.

When I did see Emma weeks later, a decorated German officer led her down the street as if he were exhibiting his latest trophy. They walked arm in arm as she glanced my way. Carefully she turned her head in the opposite direction as to not notice me for her own safety and mine as well. Obviously the decorated Nazi soldier had selected my Emma to be his wife. There was nothing either one of us could do to change her fate.

Depression filled my being after I saw Emma with the German soldier. I knew she was alive and safe, but this did not console me much. Unfortunately, I did not see her again during the war or ever know what became of my dear lady friend, and I have never forgotten her.

When the war ended a couple years later, I remained in Germany for certain reasons. I worked and searched for Emma on the streets. I could not find my friend or ever see her another time. I do not know if she survived the war. I will always have good memories of my days and hours with her. She brought me the best times of my life during the terrible war. She helped me to stay alive by her love and the food she brought me to eat. She was like an angel. Perhaps, someday we will meet again.

CHAPTER SIXTEEN

Injured at Work

The war dragged on for me especially after I lost Emma to the German officer. I could not listen to the radio now that I had also lost contact with Henry Jansen. Therefore, I did not know much about what was going on with the war after I no longer had the ability to stay informed. Not knowing how my family was doing or if they were alive worried me some days. My mom and siblings were on my mind, and I hoped and prayed they were safe. At this point in the war, the state of my mind was not too good.

Mentally, I was back in a bad situation after Emma left me. I was hungry and becoming weak. I feared I would die if I stayed at the factory much longer. I came to the conclusion I must find a way to get out of the unpleasant work at the Hermann Goering factory soon. So I took a risk and decided to try to find out if Henry was still alive.

I began to ask around the POW camp and at the factory for someone who could write a letter in German for me to send to Henry. Not knowing enough of the language prevented me from writing a letter by myself even though I had learned to speak the native tongue pretty well. My plan was to attempt to communicate with Mr. Jansen to see if he had survived the bomb blast at his residence. I would ask if I could come back to work for him if he was well and could use my help. Working for him would be much better than dying in the horrid ammunition factory.

It took me a few weeks before I found someone who was willing to take the risk and write me a letter to send to Henry. In the labor camp, finding writing paper, pens, and stamps was no easy task for a POW. After I became acquainted with a person who wrote German, I had him write Mr. Jansen and ask him to bring me back to work in the coal business. Due to the constant danger surrounding us, we had to be careful and discreet.

My writing cohort and I snuck writing utensils from the factory, and the plan I had for returning to Henry's employment came to light. Mailing the correspondence was not a problem. We were able to find a mailbox on the street on the way back to the bunker one day and mail the letter.

While I was patiently waiting to see if I would get an answer from Mr. Jansen, I had an unfortunate accident at the factory. This mishap could have been potentially fatal for me in so many ways. I had worked in the labor camp for about another month after my letter had been mailed to Henry's address when the unexpected incident at the ammunition factory occurred. One day, as I longed to hear from Henry, a hundred pound oiled and slimy artillery bullet slipped from my hands while I was working on the line. The glossy piece of artillery fell on my left big toe and crushed the digit, causing me severe pain. The bone was showing and blood squirted from my foot. I started to feel sick almost immediately.

My Nazi boss took me outside to evaluate the situation. All I remember is passing out from the pain. It was not the thing I wished would happen to get me out of work.

The next thing I could recall was waking up in an ambulance going to the hospital for treatment on my foot. I did not know where I was going or what they planned to do to me. What would stop the Germans from just letting me bleed to death? Many men had been killed for no reason at all. Now I was injured and maybe not able to work. My only hope at the time was that the medical people were not unsympathetic Nazis who would let me die.

The doctor who examined me said I had to have surgery to fix my toe. The surgeon who fixed me up was an older Russian lady doctor. My surgeon was really nice to me. Similarly, she had been taken from her home and birth family in Russia. She was seventy-three years old and a slave laborer like me. Her surgical skills were very good. The job she did on my toe was priceless to me. All the bones went back together in the big toe as they were supposed to. To this day, one can hardly tell I had a bad smash injury there except where the toenail has not grown back.

The surgeon admitted me overnight in the hospital. I endured a terrible experience staying in that Nazi German medical facility as a result. I thought I would die there during the night. I did not trust anyone since the whole country was controlled by Nazis after all.

The nurses gave me pills to make me sleep and for the pain. It was bad medicine. I was dreaming all night. I felt like someone was choking me as I slept. I couldn't breathe. I really thought I was dying. It was very frightening. Once again, I thought about my mom and how much I missed her as I tried to be calm.

I did survive the night, and in the morning, the doctor released me back to the camp. I remember the doctor who released me. His name was Dr. Show. He checked me over and told me to go back to work. I had one shoe on my good foot and a bandage on my injured foot. I had to walk two to three kilometers back to the concentration camp on my sore foot without a shoe. I remember the blood started to come through the bandage as I walked and the pain was intense.

When I arrived at the ammunition factory, the Nazi guards made me go right back to work. I was only nineteen, and so young to suffer so much. I feared for my life every day, and complaining about my suffering could get me killed. At least I got my other shoe back.

I continued to care for my toe as best I could and it healed completely. In addition to focusing on my health, I waited to hear from Henry.

CHAPTER SEVENTEEN

A Miracle Happens

Another significant day during the war occurred while I was working at the Hermann Goering ammunition factory when two men came to my job and told me to come with them. They were Gestapo officials identifiable by the uniforms they wore and the big red SS on their sleeves. I couldn't imagine what they wanted with me.

Fear gripped my entire being when I began to imagine I had done something wrong at the factory. My mind raced with ideas leading me to believe I must have made bad bullets or the work I had done had been unsatisfactory to the supervisor. There was always someone watching over me making sure I did the assigned tasks correctly.

Frazzled nerves paralyzed me briefly. I feared these soldiers had come to punish me for making rejected bullets. The ammunition machines were so worn out it would have been easy for me to make a mistake. I waited quietly for a fate I felt would inevitably be announced and not to my liking as they led me on down the long unforgiving street to my destiny.

The Gestapo men said nothing to me as they made a gesture to follow them to their jeep. The silence between us was deafening while we walked to the jeep.

The soldier in the driver's seat steered the military vehicle down the bumpy city street to my latest bedtime quarters. When we arrived at my camp, the men told me to gather whatever possessions I had stored in my bunk. Figuring they would take me to a different concentration camp where I would be punished, I didn't understand why they would have bothered to stop to get my things if I were going to be killed anyway.

After we left my camp, something really strange happened next. The men took me to a nice restaurant and I was allowed to eat whatever I wanted. They must have known I was very hungry because I could barely walk from the factory to the jeep. I was underfed and exhausted. This was such a crazy thing to happen to a POW in Nazi Germany. I figured this could have been my last meal on this earth. POWs just didn't get any such privileges in Hitler's country.

I can't tell you how happy I was to eat the good food. I didn't even care if I would be dying soon. I was so hungry. I ate and ate. As I consumed the delicious food, I began to relax. The Gestapo men just didn't seem to be mad at me. I was thoroughly puzzled.

After I finished every bite on my plate, the two Nazi soldiers took me to the train station.

What is this? I said to myself. *Where on earth am I going?* I wondered in silence.

Finally, my Gestapo chaperones told me what was happening.

"You go to Altona on the train," one of them blurted out.

What a relief! I wasn't going to die!

"Thank you, sir," I whispered in a barely audible voice and saluted them respectively. Tears came to my eyes as I realized Henry Jansen, my old boss, must have gotten the letter I wrote to him. I couldn't wait to see my old boss and his family again.

The soldiers handed me a ticket that would take me back to Altona where my previous employer would be waiting when I got off the train. Henry had come at last to save my life. He would be arriving at the train depot to pick me up according to the men who had taken care of everything for him. The Almighty God had been looking over my shoulder once again.

When I got off the train in Altona, I saw Henry walking from the depot station and glancing in the direction of those exiting the stairs of the rusty locomotive. Tears of happiness filled my eyes. I had become weak and frightened and a pale thin skeleton of the Polish young man I once was. The last several months had been especially hard on me. With the accident on my foot, losing Emma, the poor conditions in the labor camp, and very little food to eat, I was lucky to have survived. I thanked the Almighty God for this new miracle.

Henry told me he was very angry at the Gestapo for taking me away from his business. As a valuable German citizen cooperating with the Nazi Party, his importance to them allowed him to be granted special favors. By simply presenting his wishes at the German employment office, he was able to demand my return to his company. As a respected Nazi supporter official, Henry was given help to find me. When I was located at the Goering Ammunition Factory, arrangements were quickly made by him for my return to his work site.

One week after I returned to Altona, Henry had me back working full time. When I first arrived at his house, he did let me rest a little. I felt like a million bucks after some good food and sleep.

A few days after I went back to work in the coal business, Henry came to talk to me in the work shed. He said he had news from my old job and told me the ammunition plant managed by Hermann Goering where I worked when he found me had recently been totally destroyed after a bombing by Allied planes. He told me mass destruction covered the area. The entire factory exploded in the attack and mixed with the dirt of the earth. Everyone in the plant died. Nothing remained standing! If I had not left until a few days later, I could have been killed. And Emma was no longer there. I was in a miracle!

Life continued to be lucky for me. I knew I had been taken care of by angels. I also believed my mother was praying for my safety. You cannot imagine all the terrible news I heard and the horrible things I saw every day of the war, which was the worst nightmare of my life.

Henry Jansen and his family were my saviors. They didn't have to help me at all. They became like family to me. I missed my mom and my own brothers and sisters deep down to my soul. Henry, his wife, son, and daughter helped me through my sorrows every day I worked for them.

Henry had a daughter my age. I didn't see her very much until later in my life when I returned to Germany. I think Henry kept his daughter hidden for safety reasons. I certainly did not blame him for this. I realized just how special a person she was when I got to know her years after the war.

I figured Henry has treated me so well because I was like another son to him. Henry and his family were good people even though they were Nazi supporters. What else could they do? Be killed themselves?

Several years after the war, I did see Henry's wife and his daughter in Germany again. Henry had died by then. I could never dismiss his kindness to me during that horrible, horrible war when I was not much more than a boy. Even after Henry's death, I continued to send money to his daughter for her to buy flowers to put on his grave when I could not do it myself on a visit to Germany. I sent her fifty dollars on one occasion and she called me.

"Joe, the money is too much!" she cried.

I said to her sincerely, "It is not to me. After all, I did owe your dad my life!"

This might show you how fond I was of the man. Just because he had died didn't mean I would ever forget what he did for me.

Unfortunately, I could not continue to stay with Henry and his family for much longer after I got back to his place. I would still work for him, but I had to go back to a work camp to keep Henry from getting into trouble. Hitler's laws forbid Henry to keep a POW in his home, so I went back to the labor camp nearest to Henry's place at night. My being closer to him than ever before in the war felt like a safe plan for me.

Henry kept me in the camp close to him so he could prevent losing me again. I went there because I cared about him. Hiding me at his house could have been very dangerous for him. Over the war years, Hitler had become suspicious of everyone. Many were trying to kill him, and Henry had to be careful to stay trustworthy.

At the new camp, I kept to myself when I was not working. I did not bother anyone, and therefore, the Nazi guards left me alone. I was close enough to Henry's workplace to walk to work. I came home tired as always, but I was alive.

In this camp, I made a friend. He was an Italian POW. He was very nice to me. He taught me some Italian. I can still speak some Italian because of the language he taught me. Eventually, we would work together. My friend was in the same situation as me. The Nazis had forced him to come to Germany and work as a slave for them as well. We were two of many thousands sharing the same fate who all hoped to be set free from our nightmare someday soon.

CHAPTER EIGHTEEN

From Human Target to Freedom

In March of 1945, on one bright sunny day, I was given orders along with the other POWs at the labor camp not to leave for our usual worksites. Confused and somewhat afraid in my guts, I prayed for safety. As we waited in fear in the primitive barracks, before long German soldiers in army trucks loaded all the POWs from my camp in to their vehicles. They drove us to the nearest railroad depot without any explanation and from this location put everyone on an old beat-up train. Not good! Not good!

I had a bad feeling about this unusual change of events. In the back of my mind, I feared we were all being taken to the Nazi ovens to be burned to death. Perhaps Hitler no longer needed our help to win the war. We were clueless and never allowed to know the plan for us.

As the rickety old train chugged down the tracks, I thought about recent days in the labor camp and the events of usual days working for Henry. He had fed me and guaranteed my safety for as long as possible. Now I sensed something had changed in the status of the war. While I loaded the coal the last couple weeks, I could hear the bombs coming more frequently in the distance, and I wondered if this train ride had something to do with the increase in the air raids I had been hearing. The Nazis had some idea for us. Of that conclusion, I had no doubt.

As we were put on the train, I could only hope the frequency of the sound of bombs I had been hearing lately meant the Allies were getting closer. I held on to optimism they were coming to save us. Our lives may be dependent on their help.

I would soon realize why we were all being moved by this train. It appeared all POWs in custody of the Gestapo were being taken to the frontlines of the war to be targets for their enemy to provide them protection. Apparently, the Nazis were making us a safety shield for themselves. We would be lucky to live through the first storm of gunfire!

Once I figured out we were going to the war front as we traveled on the rickety train, we got close enough to hear the bomber planes approaching as the Allies engaged actively with the Germans. The sound of bombs exploding could be heard in the distance. My body froze in terror of the situation I was in.

Oh my, what was happening now! I thought about Henry. He would not know where I had gone. At this point, my life was very uncertain and fearful. I prayed for the angels to save me from the bullets.

The train shipped us to the war front toward Wittenberge between Hamburg and Berlin. While we were still on the train, the US planes targeted our transportation vehicle. We were in the path of the impending air raid between the major cities. I figured the Allies must be closing in on Berlin and the Nazis were getting worried about defeat. Their worry made us a target for the Allies in their plan to destroy Berlin. We would be used as human shields against their bullets.

When the planes started to expel missiles near the tracks, soldiers on board also began to strafe at the train. The German officers ordered the locomotive be stopped and told all prisoners to flee quickly from the train and take cover in the ditches. Everyone jumped out the huge wooden door as soon as someone slid it open and we scampered for our lives.

As I ran for the nearest ditch, a couple of times shrapnel from exploding bombs pierced the thin material of the jacket I wore. I could feel hot steel hitting my body as I was being showered with life-ending remnants of a war I did not ask to be a part of!

Soon I realized my head was bleeding, but I wasn't hurt bad enough to fall down so I just kept running away from the bombs and tried to take cover. When I reached the safety of a drench ditch, I breathed a sigh of relief and waited to see what would happen next. This awful war never seemed to end for me, and I was getting tired of trying to be strong. I had struggled for over three years to stay alive. Once again, I wondered if my efforts had all been in vain as I drifted off to sleep with the sound of bombs buzzing in my ears. I slept for what seemed like days.

Years after this terrible experience of getting caught in the middle of a bombing attack, I could still feel the scars on my head and remember the shrapnel piercing my skull. I presume other scraps of bullets must have penetrated my body in other places when a couple of years ago I started to set the alarms off in airports with routine scanning. I find it funny I really don't remember much about those scars. At the time, shock paralyzed my brain from the trauma I suffered.

When the bombing in the German countryside stopped the next day, I slept peacefully on the hard ground oblivious to my surroundings. I woke up to a quiet beautiful morning covered with dirt and blood but alive. I suppose I should have been feeling grateful for being saved from death, but actually I felt more hopeless than ever.

The German soldiers gave us work orders which detailed digging trenches to trap the Allied army tanks reported to be coming our way. However, once again the planes came back, and the German soldiers retreated to Hamburg and left us to defend ourselves. About eighty POWs took cover in an old farm near the Elbe River Channel, and the Allied Forces went off in another direction.

Surprisingly, the Allies moved away from us as if they knew the Germans had left the area. It seemed all of us POWs might be safe at the farm for a few days. No one really knew what to do because the status of the war was a puzzle to us all.

Eventually, we decided to separate to find food and shelter. Our captors were gone, leaving us to fend for ourselves. As far as we knew, all of us were now free and no longer prisoners unless the Nazis came back and recaptured us!

I lived with some of the former POWs at an uninhabited farm for several days. We had no food to eat on the abandoned farm where we took shelter until we found a potato cave after much searching for something to nourish our frail starving bodies. We lived on boiled or campfire fried potatoes while we were there and drank water from the creek. The water must have been good since we didn't get sick. Although most of us were banged up and sickly, our situation started to look better than the horrible conditions most of us had all endured for over three years.

Strangely, after months and months of terror, we felt safe on this lonely farm even with the sound of bombs in the distance. Relief was a common feeling among the group. I thanked God once again for saving my life. I prayed for the safety of my family back in the Sambor district when I had some time to breathe freely and think about them. Freedom felt wonderful yet fearful, especially if we didn't have enough food to sustain us.

Under the current circumstances, we found ourselves facing uncertainty. Our group of POWs continued to appear to be free from imprisonment since the Germans had left us at the farm and never returned. Unfortunately, we would be defenseless against any soldiers with weapons who might shoot at us. We had no guns ourselves and had never been allowed to have them of course. Our only hope was to be identified as POWs by the Allies if they found us. Certainly, our torn and tattered clothes would be a sure give away of our status in this war-ravaged countryside. Nearly all of us were gaunt and unhealthy looking. We were a pathetic sight.

One day while hiding on the farm with the other POWs, I wandered off in a field by myself looking for something to eat. I was hungry and feeling overly brave. I spotted a chicken running loose through the barren land. This fine fowl would make a good choice for my dinner. I decided to catch and roast the savory looking bird up for a meal. I ran fast and captured the slippery chicken without hesitation.

While kneeling on the ground getting ready to snap the chicken's neck and cook him for lunch, I hovered over the fat rooster anticipating a delicious meal. All at once, I felt the hair stand up on the back of my neck. I had a strange sensation I was not alone. Most certainly, my feelings were correct.

Just as I was about to strangle the chicken for my meal, the cold barrel of a rifle touched the skin near the nape of my neck. Chills sizzled down my spine.

When I looked up, there were two young German soldiers pointing their guns at my face and yelling. They could not have been much older than teenagers and only a few years younger than I was. Why they were out here in the middle of nowhere confused me.

The brazen young soldiers who found me alone and in possession of a chicken I did not own were ready to pull their triggers and end my life as they had no doubt been taught to do. All I could think of was *Not more bad luck!*

I didn't want to die this day. After all I had been through in this horrible war, I felt I had beaten the odds of dying thus far, so I prayed my life wouldn't end in such a senseless tragic way.

I raised my eyes to the heavens and silently asked God to spare my life. This was the most profound moment of the war for me. I know I had no right to ask my Lord for a favor. I was stealing meat from a farmer, and the punishment for what I had done was in the Lord's hands.

As I looked up into the calming blueness of the sky, I realized the young soldiers were still screaming. I knew nothing of the message they were trying to convey. They were talking too rapidly in German for me to understand them. I tried to make out some of their words to no avail. I remained still and silent as I waited for fate to take its course.

All of a sudden, an OSS officer appeared from nowhere. He was dressed in a German uniform and he had a kind look to his face.

What? I asked myself. *Where did he come from?*

The OSS officer dismissed the young soldiers and told them he would handle me. They saluted the man they believed surpassed them in rank and left.

I sighed silently a breath of relief. My life had been spared one more time.

The OSS officer disappeared as quickly as he had appeared. I never saw him again. I felt a miracle happened to me this day. God had other plans for me other than to die alone in this field. I often wonder if the OSS officer had been an angel sent to protect my life.

Even though my life had been spared, I wondered why the suffering continued. While in hiding on the abandoned farm, the soldiers and I had no soap. We had no clean clothes. The lice ate us up. This was no way to live, so we decided to move on. Eventually, several of the POWs began to walk to Hamburg to find work and food. We had no idea if the war was over or what had happened in Hamburg. We decided to take the chance things had improved.

I agreed with the others the time to leave our hiding place had come. I gathered what little belongings I had and any food the group had found and took off on foot back to the place where the group had come from in the labor camps.

The walk to Hamburg would be one or two days for us. We were weak and tired. Some of the men were sick. We were determined to stay together and find a better life for ourselves or die trying. To a degree, the war had made most of us insistent to survive and resilient to our hardships. Personally, I figured I had missed three birthdays and was now probably twenty-one years old.

Along the way to Hamburg, I found a refugee camp with some other POWs in Wentorf by Bergedorf. I had the opportunity to meet General George S. Patton there. Soldiers at the fireside gathering one evening told me the general was one of the greatest American officers ever to be born. Their stories made me curious about him, and I became tremendously honored when one day he walked down a path near the POWs and asked me for a favor. He wanted wooden boxes containing personal possessions and items from high ranking German officers loaded on a truck. Disbelief overcame by senses at the sound of his voice.

"Young soldier," he barked at me from a distance, "would you lend me a hand?"

I gained my composure, rose, and honorably saluted the man I revered.

"It would be my pleasure, sir," I told the general in severely broken English.

The tall and stately General George Patton walked curtly away and I never saw him again. I would never forget this day when I met one of the greatest men who helped to save my life. I learned that he died later in the year in an accident with his jeep in Germany. One day, when I was much older, I did go to see his grave while visiting the WWII American and Polish cemeteries in Luxembourg.

I didn't stay long in that camp because I heard the Polish Armed Forces Organization in Germany wanted any of the displaced POWs willing to volunteer their services in the northwest region up to the Danish border. At this point, I had no other options for my life. I would have to make plans for my employment once I arrived back in Hamburg and recovered from fatigue and malnutrition. It was my honor to serve my country in Germany for as long as they needed me to do so.

On the day I finally arrived back in Hamburg, the city remained under British occupation. I could hardly believe the sights of the city. Previously, the Nazis had taken me to the countryside in a train where I could not visualize the territory being bombed. Now I saw the German countryside in ruin and Hamburg was no better. Most of the buildings had been heavily damaged or destroyed. Words simply cannot describe the widespread destruction the bombs had caused all over the once beautiful city and countryside. Homes and businesses were burnt and charred and the smell of it all stung my nostrils.

News of the English Army liberating Hamburg and the war being over circulated the entire city. I would find out later the date to be early in May 1945 and I had been a POW for three years and six months. Amen to God. I had survived the concentration camps, the bombs, and the war. On this day, I decided it was time for me to heal and begin to put my life back together.

CHAPTER NINETEEN

Post WWII in Germany

Now that I was back safely in Hamburg, I went with other Polish POWs to find the proper authorities to ask for a job. We could all see there was an enormous amount of repair work to be done in the city. What else were we all to do? At this point, not one of us had an idea if we could go back to Poland. We didn't know if our country had survived the war and we were displaced together. Many POWs from all over Europe were in the same uncertain position. We were starving and the local military organizations offered us food and housing in exchange for work.

I didn't realize how bad of shape I was in when the Allies rescued me in Hamburg. Before I could actually consider being employed and doing physical labor again, I realized I would have to spend some time recovering from the mental and physical trauma I had suffered as a result of being a POW for so long. My body was thin, bony, and malnourished. Mentally fragile, I freaked out whenever I heard a loud noise. I needed time to heal and regain mental and physical strength. There really was no urgency in starting a job at the moment.

In 1945, after WWII ended, once again I thought about eventually going to the United States of America. I wasn't sure if I could go home to Poland and wondered if I even have a home or a family to return to. Uncertain about anything for sure, the plan I had to search out my options would be a priority. Another of my primary concerns was to find out if Henry Jansen had survived the war. I assumed he remained in hiding until he was sure he would not be accused of aiding the Nazis during the war. Henry was just a businessman who did what Hitler or his officials ordered him to do. My friend was among many fearful Germans who were uncertain of their future when the war ended. With the Nazis defeated, many people had to be careful with their own lives and blend in as normal German citizens. I just didn't know if Henry had been able to do that.

Eventually, I found my best option for employment would be to join up with the Polish Armed Services through their commander. I knew working with fellow Polish soldiers would make me feel more at home while we were stationed together in the northwest region of Germany in Schleswig Holstein. This is where I planned to enroll in Polish Driving School and learn to drive the military jeeps. There was no job I would rather do, and I was excited to have the chance to learn to operate the many large transportation vehicles of the army.

As a Polish soldier working in Germany, I was given comfortable living quarters in the barracks and generous amounts of food to eat. I became a registered ex-prisoner of war and a proud soldier of the Polish Armed Forces. The German people now treated me with due respect, and I was granted all the rights of a free citizen of their country.

After I obtained an identity card through Polish Headquarters in the Schleswig-Holstein region of the northernmost part of Germany, I could come and go freely in the area when my job duties were complete. The ID card identified me by name, fingerprint, birth date, birth place, dad's name, religion, and rank in the Polish Armed Forces. After all, there were many displaced persons to keep track of, and the cards surely helped the officials in charge to keep track of us all.

Polish Armed Forces ex-prisoner of war identity card.

Not having a birth certificate to provide the date and place of my birth proved to be a problem for identification purposes. Obtaining a new document proving my birth as soon as I could after the war would be essential for many reasons. In order to recreate the new birth certificate, I was required to provide the details of my birth to the senior Polish officer at the Polish Headquarters before I would be allowed to obtain an official driver's certificate.

The senior Polish officer accepted my birth information and I began instructions at the Polish Driving School through the Starsky Polish Office in Lubeka of the Holstein-Schleswig region of northwest Germany after I told the officer in charge of my interest in driving for them. So I learned to do my favorite job after the war and drive a jeep! After I was driving successfully and passed an examination for the officers, I received a driver's certificate in 1946. My first driver's license was German and provided for by the Polish Armed Forces Service Headquarters and included a certificate of my birth information. I was expected to get a new war department driving permit every year I drove in Germany.

MY NAME IS JOZEF BEDNARZ

German driver's certificate, side 1.

German driver's certificate, side 2 with birth information.

Once I started to drive jeeps and supply trucks in postwar Germany, I got my first wages since I left Poland. I was so happy to be alive, to have a job, and to have good army buddies who like me were taken from their homes and put in forced labor camps. They came from all over Europe. As POWs we had come together to survive and clean up the devastation Hitler had caused in Germany. Returning to our homelands was still uncertain for us.

Photo of me siting in the army jeep.

I was stationed in Northern Germany close to the North Sea. My favorite pastime when I wasn't working was to swim in the sea! After what I had been through in the war, I was in heaven as I learned to swim in the cool refreshing water of the mighty North Sea.

Laying on the beach of the North Sea in 1946.

The Polish Armed Forces were demobilized in Germany on July 6, 1947, and Great Britain assumed control of the Northeast region of the country where I was stationed. My service had to be changed over to the group 313TPT GR CLO, and I had to be approved as reliable and healthy for service under command of the English Army. After a successful interview and health exam, I told the officer-in-charge I wanted to stay a driver, and I continued to drive the jeeps doing various deliveries as I did for the Polish Army. On the day the British took over the Schleswig-Holstein region, I was issued a certificate verifying my change in service orders.

Certificate of Demobilization of the Polish Army, July 6, 1947.

Driving the army jeeps for the British was an exciting way for me to work, earn some cash, and do some good with my time while I decided how I would proceed with my life. I drove various army vehicles and delivered supplies all over northern Germany. I was given a weekly gas allowance by the officer-in-charge. I used my psychology to figure out how much gas money I needed to get through the week. I started to coast down the hills in order to save fuel. My idea was to tell the officer how much money I needed for gas doing regular driving. When I coasted with the trucks, I had gas left over at the end of the week. When the officer gave me the normal amount of gas money, I used what I needed to fill the tank and saved the rest of the money.

After a couple years of skimming off my gas allowance, I had saved quite a bit of money to help me start a new life. I knew I wanted to go to America. I wasn't sure how I would get there, but I anticipated I would need money to help me survive no matter where I settled after my time in Germany ended.

During nearly four years as a driver for the English, I enjoyed the company of many high-ranking officials. Some days, the officer-in-charge would summon me to drive a general to a specific location. I would chat with him a little and try to learn his language. Most of the generals were kind and helpful to me. I felt privileged to have been given this special opportunity in my life. I owed a lot to these men who gave me work after the war, and I treated them like kings.

After recovering from the war and getting settled in northwest Germany, the next five years of my life were spent working to gain the trust of the German government. During this time, all European POWs were listed as displaced persons with the IRO (International Refugee Organization). Early in 1949, I had informed the IRO of my intention to be placed in America. It wasn't until two years later I received an official letter dated February 8, 1949, from the United States Department of Justice, Immigration, and Naturalization Service, accepting me as a future resident of the US. The correspondence came from the commissioner of immigration who personally welcomed me to the country and advised me how to become a citizen of the US. Behind my eyes, the wheels were turning in the right direction for me to leave Germany once and for all and start a new life in America.

KATHERINE RITCHIE

UNITED STATES DEPARTMENT OF JUSTICE
IMMIGRATION AND NATURALIZATION SERVICE
WASHINGTON 25, D. C.

OFFICE OF
COMMISSIONER

PLEASE ADDRESS REPLY TO
AND REFER TO THIS FILE NO.
153/Gen.

TO OUR NEW RESIDENT:

As the Acting Commissioner of Immigration and Naturalization of the United States of America, I cordially welcome you upon your arrival.

The enclosed Alien Registration Receipt Card does not require my signature. It is a valid certification that you were admitted to the United States on the date, at the place, and in the manner indicated, and that you have been registered under the Alien Registration Act, 1940. Inquiry concerning the validity of the card is not necessary. Any change in your address should be reported to my office.

Persons who come to make their homes in this country usually wish to become citizens when they have been here long enough. An applicant for citizenship (among other requirements) must be able to speak English, to sign the petition for naturalization, and to show understanding of the principles of the Constitution and Government of the United States.

The public schools in many cities and towns have classes for applicants to learn about these subjects. They will be very glad to help you should you ever need that help. This instruction will make it easier when appearing before the naturalization examiner.

I extend best wishes for your success in your new country.

Sincerely,

[signature]

Acting Commissioner

Enclosure
E-57
2-8-49

Letter of acceptance from the United States Department of Immigration.

Eventually, the postwar repair work would be done in this part of Europe and former POWs like me who were now soldiers as well as other people who were displaced from the war would have to be dispersed somewhere else in the free world. I worked with the German ambassador, the Polish Armed Forces, and the IRO to get my papers in order to be transferred to America. I proved to my superior officers to be a good worker and they helped me to put the papers I needed together for my emigration to America. My senior officer provided an evaluation of my character to facilitate the process.

313 Tpt. Gr. CMLO

To whom it may concern.

This is to certify that No. 042029 BEDNARZ JOZEF was employed in 313 Tpt. Gr. CMLO as a DRIVER from 7.6.47 till 20.2.50.

The above named is known to me to be a sober, reliable and conscientious man.

Hamburg
Date: 15.2.50

(F. J. Stageman) Major RASC
OC 313 BSE Transport Service Group CMLO

Testimonial given by the transport service officer, February 15, 1950.

Before I could hope to leave Germany and come to America, I needed more proof I had been an honest and respectable person prior to becoming a soldier for the English Army. America would not accept criminals coming into the country. I believed Henry would be the best person I knew in Germany to swear to my good character. So I searched for Henry Jansen and finally located him in his original business location. You can only imagine my excitement at seeing him again and getting his help for immigration to the US.

Henry verified I came from Brzesciany, Poland, before the war and wrote a statement about the reliable person I had been doing forced labor for him during my imprisonment in Hamburg-Altona. This document would one day be of great importance to me in acquiring a pension I never dreamed I was eligible to receive as a POW of WWII. His testimonial proved invaluable in helping me get to America as well.

HENRY JANSEN Kohlen · Koks · Briketts
Spezialität: Zentralheizungskoks

Kontor und Lager: Bankkonten: Vereinsbank in Hamburg, Altonaer Filiale
Mörkenstraße 84-90 Norddeutsche Bank, Fil. Altona · Postscheck: Hamburg 38438
Fernsprecher: **42 48 76**

Hamburg-Altona, den _____ 195__

Henry Jansen letterhead-My boss parttime during the War

In addition to the testimonials I needed for emigration, I was required to obtain a certificate from the International Refugee Organization, similar to the US passport. The IRO worked with the eligibility officer in Osnabruck, Germany, to complete this important document for me. The testimonial he provided regarding my work and behavior while in Germany helped my case although I still needed to complete documentation regarding my birth certificate. On November 9, 1950, I made a sworn testimonial to the officer in charge of my case at the CMLO about the loss of my official birth certificate back in Poland. This document would replace my original records.

MY NAME IS JOZEF BEDNARZ

Document of sworn statement explaining
the loss of birth certificate.

After the necessary paperwork had been completed, V. M. Guillot, the eligibility officer from the IRO Field Office, granted me a certificate of eligibility as an official refugee acceptable for immigration to the US, dated November 26, 1950. Everything seemed to be falling into place for me to move to America. I could hardly believe my dream was coming true.

IRO (International Refugee Organization) certificate, front side.

After four years of service to the English Army in Germany, I was given an honorable discharge and a letter of commendation from the major who was my superior. In addition to all my other testimonials, I needed proof, as much proof as I could get, that I was not a criminal and would be considered fit for settlement in the US. This final testimonial and discharge papers completed the requirements I needed for emigration.

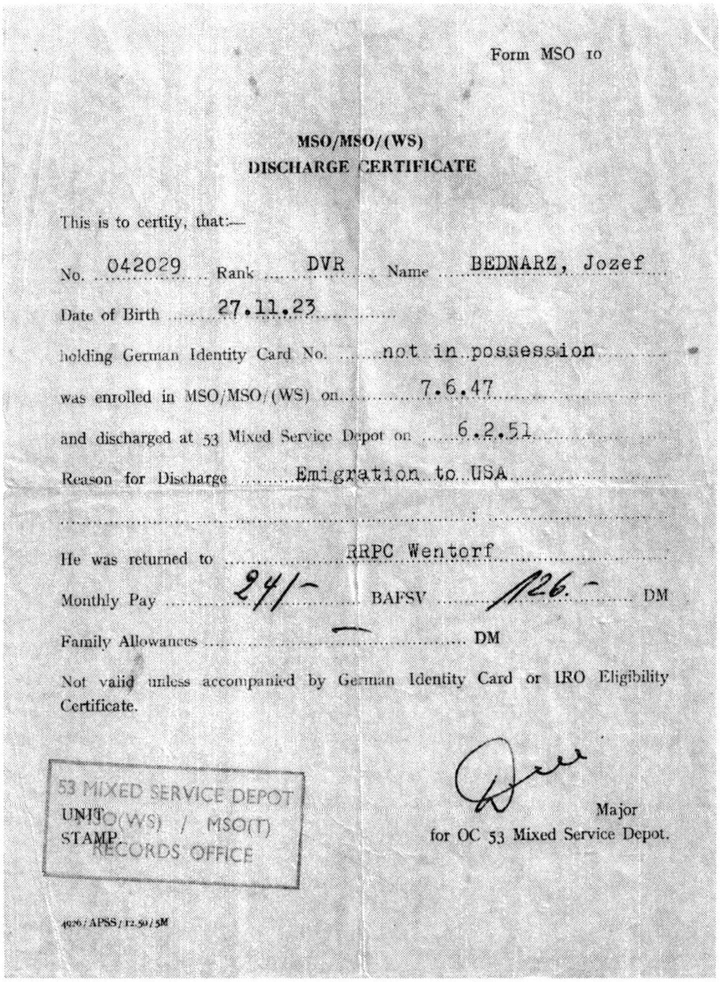

MY NAME IS JOZEF BEDNARZ

Form MSO 10

MSO/MSO/(WS)
DISCHARGE CERTIFICATE

This is to certify, that:—

No. 042029 Rank DVR Name BEDNARZ, Jozef

Date of Birth 27.11.23

holding German Identity Card No. not in possession

was enrolled in MSO/MSO/(WS) on 7.6.47

and discharged at 53 Mixed Service Depot on 6.2.51

Reason for Discharge Emigration to USA

He was returned to RRPC Wentorf

Monthly Pay 24/- BAFSV 126.- DM

Family Allowances DM

Not valid unless accompanied by German Identity Card or IRO Eligibility Certificate.

53 MIXED SERVICE DEPOT
UNIT O(WS) / MSO(T)
STAMP RECORDS OFFICE

Major
for OC 53 Mixed Service Depot.

4026/APSS/12.50/5M

Discharge certificate, dated June 2, 1951.

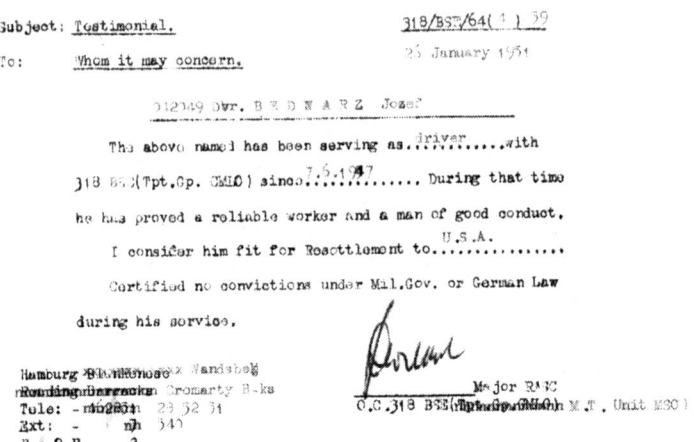

Testimonial of being fit for emigration, 1951.

Through the IRO, I acquired a resettlement director from the United States of America. He was Father Leo Berger of Saint Andrew's Catholic Church in Sibley, Iowa, USA, who would find me a sponsor before my trip from Germany to the United States of America by ship. Joseph Welp of Welp's Hatchery, Bancroft, Iowa, agreed to sponsor my employment in the US and provide the funds for inland transportation from New York, New York, by train to Fort Dodge, Iowa, USA. In exchange for their sponsorship, I agreed to work for the Welp's at the hatchery for one year.

MY NAME IS JOZEF BEDNARZ

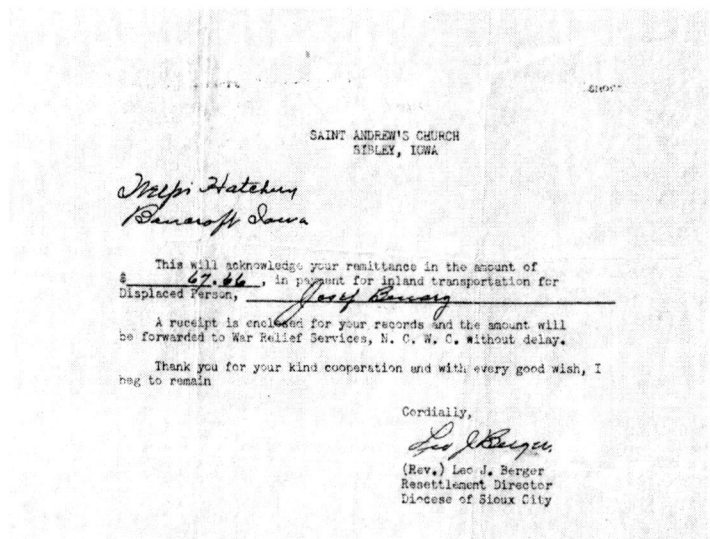

Receipt for transportation to the US from
Father Leo Berger to Welp's Hatchery.

The process for my emigration was long and difficult but eventually a success. During the first couple years after WWII, the United States had refused to take displaced persons from the war into their country. I was afraid I might have to go back to Poland and communist rule. I believe some law had passed in the late '40s in the US and immigrants were again being allowed to come into the country. When my own papers were finalized, I was so very happy to be going to America, yet afraid of the big new world.

CHAPTER TWENTY

Going to America

In March of 1951, the day had finally arrived for me to travel to America with four other Polish bachelors who would also be sponsored by Welp's Hatchery in Bancroft, Iowa. In order to get to the transport vessel to America, we had to travel by train to Bremerhaven, Germany. From there, we would sail to the USA on a big ship with about five hundred other European persons displaced by the war who were also immigrating to the US.

Our journey to America started in the seaport city of Bremerhaven, Germany, on the banks of the North Sea, which eventually led to the massive Atlantic Ocean and the promising lands of the USA. We boarded the USAT *M. B. Stewart*, a transport ship authorized to bring displaced persons from Europe to their new homeland. The huge boat was formerly an official US Navy transport ship in WWII named in honor of US Army general Merch Bradt Stewart. Between 1950 and 1955, she carried thousands of European refugees to the United States and Canada under the International Refugee Organization. I was told she could actually accommodate up to three thousand troops during wartime.

The trip across the Atlantic Ocean in the huge seaworthy vessel was another exciting adventure for me. By now, I was twenty-seven years old! It had been nearly ten years since the Nazis took me from my home and I had seen my family. I knew in my heart life would get better, and I believed I would see my family once more even though the communists had taken over our beloved Poland. I assumed my family had suffered in many ways from the war, and I prayed for them every day. But for now, I had to survive yet another dangerous escapade in crossing the big ocean before I could be safe and assured starting a new life in America was my destiny. Then one day, in the future, I would hopefully see my family again.

The journey on the giant seaworthy ship proved quite bumpy. Gigantic waves rocked her bow and stern on many days. For the most part, I had a great experience traveling on the high seas once I got used to the constant movement of the boat while many other passengers hung their heads over the side of the boat to throw up.

The food on the boat could not have been much better. We were given fresh fruit to eat and bottles of Coke among other things I had not tasted in years if ever. I had a bed to sleep in and I felt relatively comfortable especially after sleeping in barracks for the last nine plus years. The valuable life I had so strongly sheltered since I left Poland by force seemed to be safe in the hands of the ship's crew.

Through all of the hardships I suffered in my life, I never forgot the Almighty Father who had allowed me to survive those times including the nearly four years I spent as a POW. During my voyage to America, I had no idea of His plan for me. At this point in time, I couldn't wait to see America and how my journey on this earth would continue.

The long trip brought on boredom for me as we cruised across the rebellious Atlantic Ocean. I had been cleaning sleeping quarters and scrubbing the deck on occasion, and before long, these chores came to completion. After a couple of hours with nothing to occupy my time, I asked the crew if I could help out in other ways, and they obliged. I was given a special job to do, and from there on out, I spent much time painting walls and sprucing up the ship in order to repay my gratitude to them for allowing me to be on their mighty vessel.

After several days, we arrived in the harbor of New York City, New York, and beheld a beautiful sight! I walked out on the deck to see the Statue of Liberty, which was the most incredible statue I had ever seen in my entire life. I stood at the bow of the ship and just stared at her in awe. I imagined the beautiful lady on the island in the bay to be holding up her gleaming light to welcome me to my dreams. I had made it to America and tears came to my eyes. After waiting for over twenty years to come to this country, I felt overwhelmed with emotion having accomplished the vision I had dreamed of since I was a child.

I could hardly believe I was actually standing before America's most prized possession. The Statue of Liberty stood right in front of my eyes as if she had waited for me to arrive. The Lady of America was beautiful. My childhood dreams were now a reality and I cried.

Once the ship docked in New York Harbor, we were shuttled by ferry to Ellis Island. All foreigners had to sign their names in a big book and register to be immigrants to the United States of America. As we wrote our names in the great ledger, we made history for ourselves. I for one could not have been more proud to be registered as an emigrant to the United States of America with my signature and birth date recorded at Ellis Island on March 21, 1951.

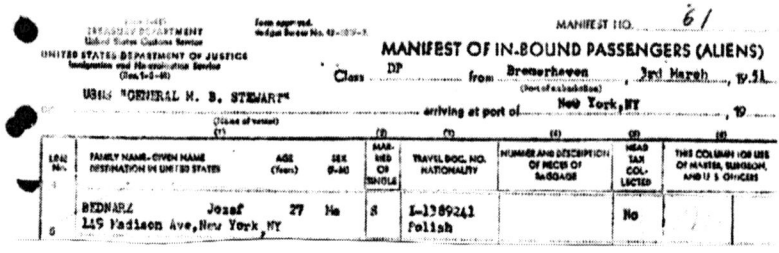

New York passenger list for the *M. B. Stewart*, March 1951.

Before continuing on the journey to our final destinations, all passengers had to have a brief medical exam and our legal immigration papers were verified. Due to the large number of immigrants, the required formalities consumed much time, and we simply had to endure the long hours of waiting our turns. Some people were kept in housing complexes overnight waiting for their turn and others were kept at infirmary facilities until they were healthy enough for more travel. Fortunately, my travelling Polish companions and I had all our necessary documents in order as well as being healthy, and we were cleared for admittance into the country. Soon enough, we were on our way, and to my surprise, I was given a letter of welcome from the US Displaced Persons Commission before I left New York.

DISPLACED PERSONS COMMISSION
WASHINGTON 25, D.C.

Dear Sir or Madam:

    The Displaced Persons Commission welcomes you to the United States of America.

    The Congress of the United States of America has established the Displaced Persons Commission to select for immigration to this country, persons displaced as a result of World War II. Under the principles laid down by the Congress, you are among those selected.

    The Congress is interested in how displaced persons fare after settling in the United States. So that the Congress may be kept informed on this matter, it requires that each person who immigrated to the United States as the head of a family or as a single person provide certain factual information.

    The information is to be provided twice a year, for two years. The reporting dates are July 1 and January 1. The first report is required on the next reporting date after you have been in the country 60 or more days. Each of the reports must be in the mails to reach us by the date specified, but may be mailed as much as fifteen days earlier.

    The form for reporting is provided by the Displaced Persons Commission. The form to be used will be available on May 15 for the July 1 report and on November 15 for the January 1 report. It will be available at local offices of the U. S. Immigration and Naturalization Service.

    The Displaced Persons Commission wishes you every success in your new life in the United States of America.

                                    Sincerely,

                                    Ugo Carusi, Chairman
                                    Edward M. O'Connor
                                    Harry N. Rosenfield

DPC 219
2-15-59

Letter of Welcome from Displaced Persons Commission, Washington, DC.

The journey to our new home resumed on a train from New York to Fort Dodge, Iowa. My fellow Polish bachelors and I traveled in March and the late winter weather was unpredictable much as it had been in Poland and Germany. When we got to Chicago, the snow was so deep on the tracks that the train got stuck. The cold and icy impediment to our travel had to be cleared from the tracks for hours as we waited patiently for our trip to continue. No matter. I slept in my seat just happy to be in America.

Once we got to Nora Springs, Iowa, and quite close to our final destination, the train tracks once again became impassable. We were delayed several hours in blizzard conditions waiting for our path to be cleared. I spent a lot of time sleeping when the train was not moving since there were no constant bumps to keep me awake. Resting was easier for me on the train than it had been on the ship. I felt like I hadn't slept in years when I finally got into a deep sleep. I didn't realize I probably had not achieved a good night's rest since I had been a teenager back in Poland.

Joseph Welp, the owner of Welp's Hatchery and our new boss, greeted me and the four Polish bachelors I travelled with from Germany at the Fort Dodge, Iowa, train station. He arrived to escort us the final sixty miles to Bancroft, Iowa, and the homes where we would now reside for at least a year. A stop was made in Algona, Iowa, where we met with the local staff of the *Algona Upper Des Moines* newspaper. A photographer took our picture and a reporter wrote down our unusual story on a notepad in preparation for publishing a final edition. Suddenly, we became famous for a day at least.

The *Algona Upper Des Moines* newspaper article, April 5, 1951, page 8: "5 Polish Bachelors Arrive."

In March of 1951, I arrived in a strange town with four other previous POWs from Poland to work at Welp's Hatchery. After we entered the quaint town of Bancroft, Iowa, with a population of less than a thousand people, all of us were taken to homes to live in while we were employed there. I was set up at the boarding house of Mary Lieurance, and she welcomed me with open arms. I felt right at home with her the moment I arrived.

In Mary's home, I found my living quarters to be neat and clean and adequate. The town itself was small and peaceful and just perfect for me. I felt my body and soul begin to relax the first night I spent in Bancroft.

Mary was a wonderful lady who was probably about my mother's age. I came to love her like my own mom. She fed me wonderful food, did my laundry, and helped me with the English language. Her husband passed away some years previously, and she had only one son who supported her a great deal. Running the boarding house was the way she made enough money to support herself and her son.

I started my new job at the hatchery as soon as I was settled into Mary's home. Since I had grown up and worked on two farms, I felt relatively sure I could handle the work. What I did not understand was the agreement arranged for me by the IRO and my employer. Even though Welp's Hatchery had sponsored my emigration to America, and I made a promise to work for them one year in repayment of the cost of transportation from New York, they took money out of my first six paychecks and subtracted this amount from the balance they paid for my train ride from New York to Fort Dodge. Although my money situation was not too good at first, I was grateful in so many ways for how I now lived freely in America.

```
Deducted from check to apply on receipt shown on
opposite side:

May  26, 1951                    12.50
June  2, 1951                    12.50
June  9, 1951                    12.50
June 16, 1951                    12.50
June 23, 1951                    12.50
June 30, 1951                     5.16
                                 67.66

Paid in full to Welp's Hatchery, Bancroft, Iowa.

                      B. W.

Thank you.
```

Receipt of payment in full to Welp's Hatchery
for ground transportation to Iowa.

During the year I worked at the hatchery, I endured much hardship and prejudice at Welp's, but I kept my promise to them and continued employment with them for a year. One of my supervisors yelled at me constantly and called me "a f—ing Polack." He told me to go back to Poland many times. I tried to ignore his mean words and do my job. The problem with my job at the hatchery was that I didn't always like the work I was ordered to do. I just did my best and waited patiently for the time to pass. Ironically, years later, I lived with my new family right next door to him and our children played joyfully together for many years.

Of the five emigrant Polish bachelors sponsored by Welp's Hatchery to come from Germany, I was the only one who actually did work for the entire year. I repaid my debt to them for I believed I owed the company my repayment for their sponsorship and working a year was the right thing to do. Before long, I learned to enjoy other activities in the town other than just work.

The job at Welp's required an early morning arrival. The supervisors expected me to be at the plant by seven every day. I put in the eight hours expected of all employees, and when I got back to Mary's place at the end of my shift, I would sit out on the side porch enjoying the fresh air. This was about the time the Catholic school dismissed the students two blocks away as I cast my cares into the beauty of spring in the Midwestern United States. I enjoyed relaxing in the warm breeze while watching the children go by and wondered what they had learned on this day. Sometimes, I missed my own siblings as I observed the kids going by the house. By now, even my youngest brother Mattias would no longer be in school. For a while at least, I had forgotten about the pressures of the hatchery work, lost in my thoughts.

CHAPTER TWENTY-ONE

A New Family- A New Life

As I watched the children walking by my perch at Mary's house after work, I began to notice a pretty young woman riding on her bicycle by the house every day when I sat on the porch in the chair Mary had given me to recline in after work. I observed the young woman had light brown hair. She was short in stature and of medium build. When she would look my way and smile, her face warmed my heart. I found myself curious about her. So, I waved at her one day.

The next day, I made a welcoming motion at the friendly appearing woman who crossed my path most days. Finally, she came over to say hello and we began to get acquainted. She told me she lived over on the next block with her parents and four siblings. Her name was Leanne. She was also the oldest child in her family as I had been. Immediately we discovered we had a little something in common. It seemed our new found friendship was off to a good start

Picture of Leanne.

Unfortunately, my English was very bad therefore Leanne and I could not always understand each other. Her patience with me helped to break the communication barriers we had. Eventually, we decided we discovered a common interest with dancing and Mary had told me about a place we could go. I invited her to attend a ball with me on a Saturday night. Since I had no transportation, Mary took us to the dance in Estherville, Iowa and Leanne was surprised when we pulled up to our destination. She thought we were going to a ball game as she had misunderstood me due to our language barrier.

Leanne informed me the town of Bancroft had a Ballroom. Dances were held on a regular basis on Saturday evenings in this small interesting town. Leanne's parents came to know and trust me with their daughter so we attended the weekend dancing event held in town quite often after our first date there. We went to other dances all over the area and became better acquainted.

Leanne was a senior in high school when we first met. She graduated a couple months after we became acquainted. She told me she wanted to be an artist. In the summer, she would be continuing her college studies at home that she had already begun as a high school student. I liked her and agreed to continue my courtship with her after I finished my year at Welp's.

Leanne started to work at the Bancroft Register after she graduated and I continued to fulfill my obligation at Welp's Hatchery for the remainder of the year. Once I completed the year I was glad to tell all my bosses goodbye and move on to a new location. I knew some of my Polish friends I met on the M.B. Stewart ship had moved to St. Paul and were encouraging me to come up and work for a while. Since Leanne was busy with her studies and job, I took the opportunity to travel up north and spend time with my friends.

I relocated to the Twin Cities and went looking for work. I found a job in St. Paul, Minnesota, and worked in the Schmidt Brewing Company. I visited Leanne back in Bancroft whenever I could. I enjoyed my new residence in the Minnesota city and attended St. Casimir's Catholic Church on the weekends when I was in town. The church was located in a Polish community close to where I lived. I felt connected to Poland there and found many people who spoke my language who I could communicate with along with my other friends.

I stayed only a few months in St. Paul and moved back to Iowa because I missed Leanne and was tired of driving back and forth to see her. My life choices were changing and I thought about settling down and having a family.

Once Leanne completed her studies and I had moved back to Iowa we made a decision to look for jobs in Fort Dodge, Iowa. I moved first where I found employment working for the city and lived in an apartment with my friend Peter Cuicyk. Leanne came to live in Fort Dodge a few months later and was hired at the Bell Telephone Company. Our relationship grew to the point we decided to marry.

Leanne Marlow and I were married in her home parish church of St. John the Baptist in Bancroft on July 6, 1953. Nineteen years later we were the proud parents of twelve children living back in Bancroft, Iowa, USA. My life was truly blessed. Thanks to God!

Our Wedding picture with Leanne's
Grandparents (The Marlow's)

Becoming a US citizen was necessary for me to live in America so I began my studies with Leanne's help after we married. On April 12, 1957, while Leanne was five months pregnant with our third child, Janice, I became a proud citizen of the United States of America.

Certificate of Naturalization

I went back to Poland and the town of Klodzko to see my family in 1964 for the first time after I had been taken from them all by the Nazi's in 1941. By then, I was already married with seven children of my own and living in Fort Dodge, Iowa. My birth family lived in Klodzko, Poland. Since the borders of Poland had changed as a result of Communist rule, my family had been forced to migrate to southwestern Poland. When the Russians took over the eastern third of Poland after WWII, Brzesciany had become a part of Ukraine. The good news for me was that my family was alive and safe. They had also survived WWII!

Poland had remained under Communist rule since WWll when I returned in the spring of 1964 and left my wife in charge of our seven children for one month. There was still a lot of fear of the government in my country in those days. The Communists were everywhere and they ruled everything. Soldiers carried machine guns at the airport when I arrived. I felt like I was constantly being watched because I was an American of Polish descent however nothing could spoil the great excitement I had in my heart in anticipation of seeing my beloved family again.

My return to Poland in 1964 with possibly Piotr Bednarz son of Stanley in the background

When I went to my parent's home in Klodzko, I found out my dad had already died in 1956 from bad alcohol when my daughter Kathy was born. My mom, who was quite a bit younger than dad had been, was still alive and well. She cried so hard to see me again when I finally came back to her. I was happy to see my mom after all I had suffered in the war, moved to America, and was married with a family. After so many years of not seeing her, I also cried and cried to see her.

I stayed in my home country for about four weeks on this first trip for me back to Poland after the war. I had a wonderful time seeing all my relatives. I would return to Poland once more with Leanne in 1974 before my mom passed away. She died in February of 1975 of old age. Over the years, whenever I went back to see my family we had a grand celebration the entire time I was there and leaving became more difficult each time. I especially hated to leave my family and go home the first time I returned. Nevertheless, I had my own life and family back in the United States and I did miss my wife and my kids immensely when I left them.

I was sad I could not stay permanently in Poland anymore. Even if I wanted to live there, the Communists would make my life miserable and I would be a prisoner once again. I felt like I was split in half between my two families after going back to Poland and renewing the relationships I had with all my blood relatives. I knew I would always be far away from my dear mother and siblings when I went back to the USA. I did know I would return whenever I could but my life would never be the same after I came to live in America. I had survived being the prisoner of a horrific war. Now, I would raise and protect my family from the hate and harm I had endured. I would teach them about God. We would go to Mass and sit in the front pews of our Catholic Church and give thanks to Him for our lives and my survival as a POW in WWII.

EPILOGUE

My father passed away before I could finish his story. He died on a snowy Monday evening in January, two months after he was diagnosed with multiple areas of cancer. He had a hard time believing cancer would take him. Dad was pretty sure he would live to be at least ninety. I believe he thought he was invincible.

When the doctor told me Dad had terminal cancer, he had also been told but the words didn't sink in. So he had to be told again.

My sister, Barb, and I sat with my father a couple days after the doctor gave us his diagnosis. We had to make him understand, so he could prepare himself for leaving this earth. Telling Dad he was dying certainly was one of the hardest things both of us had ever done. We knew he wanted to live a longer life, and this was now impossible unless God miraculously cured him.

Dad lived two months from the day he was diagnosed with the cancer. Ironically, he had been spared an extended time of suffering. He had suffered enough throughout his lifetime.

Four days before my father passed away, I called him to ask a question about his story for my book. He gave me an answer, although he was evasive about his answer. He was usually willing to help me get the story right. This day he answered my question saying, "It doesn't matter." He was normally more receptive to my questions. I should have known something was about to happen to him.

When Dad was diagnosed with cancer, my other nine living siblings were all informed of his illness. All of them had the opportunity to say their goodbyes to him. Yes, my parents had twelve children—nine girls and three boys!

A week after our talk with Dad, Barb and I prepared a wonderful Thanksgiving meal for him and celebrated his eighty-eighth birthday on Sunday. The next day he was put on hospice. His doctor and the hospice nurses would do their best to keep him comfortable until he died.

Two days after his eighty-eighth birthday, my sister, Peg, took Dad to the nearest casino to play his favorite penny slot machine as a gift from her. She couldn't get him out of the casino for four hours and the excursion was more than his sickened body could handle. The next day he ended up in the hospital for a week with a respiratory infection. In spite of having to be hospitalized, he had had a blast with his daughter at the casino and gave her memories she would always treasure.

While Dad was in the hospital, I spent three days with him. I stayed night and day taking only an occasional break. It was the least I could do to ease his suffering from the respiratory illness he came down with. I loved him, and as a nurse, I did whatever I could to anticipate his medical needs. I kept him company and made him comfortable while I was there.

While Dad was hospitalized, my sister, Theresa, came from Colorado to visit him. He was overjoyed to see her. He stood silently and just smiled when she walked into his hospice room at the hospital. He had a way of standing quiet and smiling softly when he was pleased. At this time, he was probably contemplating one of the last times he had seen her. He had shared wonderful times with her family three years previously when he flew to Colorado for her youngest daughter's wedding.

Two days later, after Theresa arrived, John, who was son number one (as Dad called him), came to stay with Dad at the hospital. Dad was proud of John and his business and family accomplishments. John had always been very special in my dad's life. His concern for Dad's health increased once he spent a few hours with Dad at the hospital. I knew he would watch over Dad. So John relieved me, and I went home to Branson, Missouri.

John stayed night and day with Dad at the hospital as I had done until he was released to the nursing home a couple days later. Dad had been living with my older sister, Barb, but she could no longer care for him. Having my brother John stay at the hospital meant the world to my dad and to my brother as well and helped with his transition to the nursing home.

I was still at the hospital with Dad when Angie flew home to see him. For financial reasons, she had not been home from Arizona in over ten years. My dad called her his angel. He started to sing to her when she walked into his hospital room. Tears came to my eyes as I watched the two of them embrace. Years apart had not been an issue for either of them to reunite.

As soon as Angie finished her visit, Jan showed up from California. She missed Dad more than any of us kids did. Dad had lived in the Palm Springs area near Jan for twelve years before he came back to Iowa. He moved back to Iowa two years previously when he felt he could no longer live alone. Jan was there for Dad when he needed her help the last several years. Back in California, she missed him terribly. She cried when she left his hospital room and went back to California knowing she would probably never see him alive again. Since he moved away from California, she missed him dearly especially during the holidays.

Mary called Dad to wish him well. She was his first daughter to become a doctor. Mary became a chiropractor a few years ago and my dad boasted about her every chance he got. Words could not adequately describe the pride my father felt in having not one but two daughters who were doctors. Sandy, the second youngest child and one of twins, also became a chiropractor. Having daughters who were doctors was a foreign concept in Poland, which made my dad inconceivably proud to have two who were.

Mary chose to remember Dad when he was healthy. That was OK because as far as he was concerned, she was there half of the time anyway. You see, Dad thought I was Mary many times. On Thanksgiving, he told me Kathy was coming to dinner thinking I was Mary. Because of our similarity in physical appearance, as far as he knew, Mary had already been there to see him.

Tom was around much of the time to see Dad. He was Dad's mechanic son. Dad was proud of Tom's knowledge of cars and how he could fix anything that needed repair. Tom took Dad to the casinos his share of the time. Dad was also proud of Tom's son, Cody. Tom had done a great job of raising Cody, and my dad told him so often.

Sandye and Sharon were Dad's twin babies of the family. The two of them spent many hours with Dad during the last six weeks of his life at the nursing home. The girls lived in Britt, Iowa, where Dad resided at West View Care Center until his death. Sharon went to see Dad almost every day, and when he passed away, both Sandye and Sharon and their families were with Dad as he slipped into a coma a couple hours before he took his last breath. I believe they helped ease the pain he suffered with their love and kindness to him. They were four years old when Dad left Iowa and moved to California. These last six weeks allowed them invaluable time to spend with Dad.

My sisters, Barb and Peggy, lived in Algona where Dad spent the last eighteen months of his life before he went to the nursing home. Barb took on the greatest challenge and took him into her home for twelve months with herself and her husband. Dad really appreciated living with his daughter, which he saw as a normal Polish tradition for aged and ill parents. When Dad's safety and health became an issue, other arrangements had to be made. Dad quickly adjusted to nursing home life as he dearly loved his nurses and assistants.

My brother Rob preceded my dad in death in September of 2007. Rob died suddenly of a probable cardiac arrhythmia caused by the flu and a minor heart infection. He was thirty-nine. My father was devastated when Rob died. Dad never really got over his death. He had spoken to my brother Rob on the phone just two days before he died unexpectedly. They were close and I believe Rob was there in heaven to greet my dad on his arrival.

My father was diagnosed with cancer November 21, 2011. He did not suffer long. He died on January 23, 2012, just before midnight after a few hours of being comatose. He died in peace. I believe he was surrounded by angels when he passed away. He had described people sitting near him who were invisible to everyone else two weeks before he died. He deserved a quiet serene passing!

Jozef Bednarz was my dad. This was his story. I hope you found hope in his story. He would have smiled with his beautiful and gracious Polish smile knowing his story was finally told.

ACKNOWLEDGMENTS

The credit for the completion of this story goes to my father, Jozef Bednarz. Without his persistence and cooperation in telling the story of his life, this book would not have been possible. To my husband, I express my gratitude for your patience with me over the seven years it took to finish the project and in dealing with my computer illiteracy. To my child, Aryn, I am so happy for your love and support and for helping me remember Dad's comments and aspects of the stories he told us both. To my stepson, Bob, I thank you for your love and support also and for treating my father like he was your own biological grandfather.

I thank my siblings: Barb Goecke, Jan Christensen, John Bednarz, Angie Curell, Theresa Gerdis, Dr. Mary Palmer, Peggy Shellenberg, Rob Michael Bednarz, Tom Bednarz, Dr. Sandye Bednarz, and Sharon Stromer, along with their spouses, significant others, children, grandchildren, and stepchildren for any time you may have helped stimulate my brain and allowed me to recall key aspects of the story of Dad's life.

And to my mother, Leanne, you helped me immensely in recalling events in Dad's life and for the great artistic talent you used to do sketches for the book in spite of your being divorced from my dad and offering no resistance to my requests for help. Thank you for being present with your children at our father's wake and funeral after his death to support us. You are a special mom and lady.

Others needing mention for my thanks are: John Carpenter for his demographic work on the images used for the book, the *Algona Upper Des Moines* newspaper for the use of the newspaper article and picture and especially to Linsday who researched the archives and got me a better copy to use for my book, the Ozark Writers League members who critiqued my work a couple times and gave me great constructive criticism, and to everyone who offered their help and listened to Dad's story and offered me encouragement.

To my friends: Gwen Plano, Michelle Peters, Debbie Harding, Dennis and Debbie Labanaski, Suzie Guymon, and everyone else who offered me invaluable support in this endeavor. Thanks to Judy Hayes for professionally scanning the documents at Staples. Finally, thanks to God for protecting my dad's life during the war and throughout his life.

ABOUT THE AUTHOR

Katherine M. (Bednarz) Ritchie was born in Fort Dodge, Iowa, to Jozef and Leanne (Marlow) Bednarz and after age eight grew up in Bancroft, Iowa. She is the second of twelve children—nine girls and three boys. She learned to be a responsible daughter at an early age. Similar to her father in some ways, she earned scant wages doing chores for her grandparents, babysitting, and working in a nursing home at the age of sixteen. She attended nursing school at Iowa Central Community College in Fort Dodge and attained her ADN (associate degree in nursing). At the age of forty, Katherine completed further nursing education and received her BSN (bachelor's degree in nursing) at Metropolitan State University in St. Paul, Minnesota. Her nursing career has spanned forty years in various areas of healthcare.

After traveling to Poland with her father in 1995, Katherine became interested in her father's life as a WWII Polish POW of which he had previously talked very little. When her dad moved back to Iowa from California after thirty-three years, he began to share the details of his life with her, and then the project of writing her first book, *My Name is Jozef Bednarz: Memoir of a WWII POW*, became a reality.

Katherine is married and lives in Branson, Missouri, with her husband Bruce and her son, Aryn, when he is home from college. She has a stepson, Bob, who lives in a group home in Iowa due to a handicap from birth. Bruce and Katherine are devout Catholics who are involved in several ministries in their parish, Our Lady of the Lake Catholic Church, in Branson. Currently, she volunteers in a free clinic for people who are less fortunate financially and have no health insurance. She is thankful to the Lord for all his blessings upon her and her family and the help received from many people to complete this work about her father's life.

CPSIA information can be obtained
at www.ICGtesting.com
Printed in the USA
FFOW02n2033010418
46132374-47216FF